DISCIPLES

ORDINARY PEOPLE
in
Extraordinary Times

Kenneth R. Overberg, S.J.

lectio

Lectio Publishing, LLC
Hobe Sound, Florida, USA

www.lectiopublishing.com

ISBN 978-1-943901-08-1
Library of Congress Control Number: 2018955945

Published by Lectio Publishing, LLC
Hobe Sound, Florida 33455
www.lectiopublishing.com

DEDICATION

Arthur J. Dewey
Scholar and Wordsmith,
Colleague and Friend

CONTENTS

INTRODUCTION

"I came so that they might have life
and have it more abundantly."

JOHN 10:10

"Beloved, let us love one another, because love is of God;
everyone who loves is begotten by God and knows God.
Whoever is without love does not know God,
for God is love.
In this way the love of God was revealed to us:
God sent his only Son into the world
so that we might have life through him."

1 JOHN 4:7-9

Jesus said to Philip, "Follow Me."

JOHN 1:43

What does it mean to be a follower of Jesus in today's world? What is discipleship? Gustavo Gutierrez offers the beginning of a response to these questions: "Discipleship is rooted in the experience of an encounter with Jesus Christ." After an introductory chapter that describes the challenge of authentic discipleship, the book presents the person and ministry of Jesus as the foundation and reason for discipleship, with special emphasis on God's overflowing love. Then it develops various aspects of the moral-spiritual life, the life of discipleship, in the midst of the blessings and challenges of everyday lives. Some of those blessings include the wisdom of the scriptures, the grace of Eucharistic celebrations, and the many areas of renewal begun in Vatican II. Some of the challenges include relativism and indifference, poverty and sickness, violence and war, suffering and death.

Disciples: Ordinary People in Extraordinary Times is a collection of a number of articles on a variety of biblical and ethical themes. Many of these articles come from *Spirituality* and *Catholic Update*. From this mosaic of articles emerges a portrait of the faithful disciple in the twenty-first century.

This book, solid theology in a readable style, invites readers into deeper insight, prayer, discussion, and action. It will be useful for individuals and parish groups such as RCIA, Mystagogy, Vincent de Paul, Christian Life Communities, and Just Faith. With profound trust and great hope, *Disciples: Ordinary People in Extraordinary Times* offers light for following Jesus.

CHAPTER 1

Examining Our Convictions

Discipleship as a Matter of Choice

Everyday life and events in our Church and world raise profound challenges for our living as faithful disciples of Jesus. What does the Gospel mean for raising children in a culture of violence or caring for aging parents and grandparents? What about economic pressures, sudden sickness, or end-of-life ethics? How do we faithfully continue Jesus' mission in the midst of terrorism and war, abuse of all kinds, polarization and pain?

Our Scriptures urge us to discern what is of value and to live according to these convictions. But what really are our deepest values and convictions? The practice of examining one's conscience is a necessary and very helpful tradition. This first chapter is an invitation to dig even more deeply, to examine the values and convictions that form the foundation of the conscience's decisions.

Perhaps an example can help here. When the United States responded to the attacks of 9/11 with war against Afghanistan, numerous bishops in the United States said that the war was regrettable but justified. Bishops from other countries around the world concluded that it was not a just war. How could this division be so clear? (There were, of course, exceptions.) Surely they all had prayed with the Gospels. Surely they all had studied the just war theory with its careful distinctions. Had some unexamined conviction determined (or at least colored) which way the search for truth would go? Did the judgment about this war being just or not rest on location or some form of nationalism?

These unexamined convictions actually shape the work of conscience, the search for the truth. They deserve, then, careful examination.

The thought of Karl Rahner, S.J., offers some guidance. In his *Theological Investigations XVIII*, Rahner points to what he calls "global prescientific convictions," unexamined assumptions, mostly cultural in character, that shape moral views and analyses.[1] These prejudgments mold people's moral imaginations and perceptions of basic values, sometimes making it difficult to live Gospel values. Everyone receives many messages that contradict the Gospel, from media and politics, business and families. One's vision of life and responses to world events often are based on these values rather than on the Scriptures and Christian tradition.

In other words, in some situations for some Christians, another set of values and convictions becomes more important than the Gospel. Often the individuals are not really aware of what is happening, for the values are rooted in unexamined assumptions, in what another author calls "unconsciously absorbed prejudices."[2]

Another example from another war. As the United States prepared for the war against Iraq, Pope John Paul II was very outspoken in his opposition. In his address to the Diplomatic Corps, for example, the pope said; "War is not always inevitable. It is always a defeat for humanity." Solutions in the Middle East "will never be imposed by recourse to terrorism or armed conflict, as if military victories could be the solution."[3] The Vatican urged the United Nations to work for a diplomatic resolution and to explore all possibilities for a peaceful settlement. Other Vatican officials commented that provision for preventive war is found neither in the *Catechism* nor in the United Nations Charter.

Still, polls showed that U.S. Catholics were in favor of a unilateral assault on Iraq by a margin of two to one. How is it that so many U.S. Catholics chose to follow the president rather than the Pope? Was some unexamined value at work, encouraging people to find the rhetoric of media and politicians more convincing than the Sermon on the Mount?

Long ago, Jesus and then later communities addressed the very same tensions and challenges. Jesus lived in an occupied land. There was no doubt who had the power. As a vivid reminder, the Roman fortress in Jerusalem overlooked the Temple area. The imperial buildings at Tiberias, not far from Nazareth and Capernaum, also attested to this power. The empire of Rome was a dominating presence.

Because of his profound, intimate experience of the God he called *Abba*, Jesus wanted others to know God's loving presence in their lives. He called this presence the reign of God. In word and deed, Jesus proclaimed its characteristics: compassion and forgiveness, service and nonviolence, faithful love. Jesus turned expectations upside down, declaring as blessed the people at the bottom of the power pyramid, the poor and marginalized (SEE LUKE 6:17-49; MATT 5:1-7:29).

We have so long prayed about the "kingdom of God" (or more recently "reign" or "dominion") that we risk domesticating the term, reducing it to a pious concept. So, to remind us of the range of Jesus's vision, some scripture scholars have suggested an alternate translation: the empire of God. In the context of the dominating power of the empire of Rome, Jesus' life and message about the empire of God necessarily had social, political and economic implications. His hearers, of course, recognized this immediately.

After the death and resurrection of Jesus and the destruction of Jerusalem years later, Luke emphasized the challenge of discipleship for his community. Luke's Jesus states: "If any man comes to me without hating his father, mother, wife, children, brothers, sisters, yes and his own life too, he cannot be my disciple. . . . So, in the same way, none of you can be my disciple unless he gives up all that he has" (LUKE 14:25-33).

As Scripture scholar Arthur Dewey points out, the harshness of Jesus' demands bothers us, even when we remember that such language was typical of religious leaders in the ancient world. "The demand that the disciple renounce even family and friends meant that he was to make a total commitment, one that placed him outside the usual behavior and customs of society."[4] Jesus summoned his followers to a new and different vision of reality, one that challenged basic assumptions of everyday life. The presence of God's reign ("empire") transformed commonly accepted values. "To follow Jesus meant to live out this new understanding of God's rule."[5]

Dewey concludes his reflections on this demanding passage: "For Luke, discipleship is a matter, not of habit or upbringing, but of choice... behavior, relationships, hopes, and dreams are also involved in the decision. To enter into the vision of God's rule is to accept God as sovereign over all, especially over what is deepest in the heart."[6]

Like Jesus and Luke and his community, we too live in an empire of dominating power. Its values have seeped into our schools, churches, businesses, families and even our own hearts. In our Baptism, however, we are called and sent out, like the early disciples, to proclaim an alternate vision: the empire of God, with its compassion and nonviolence and love, with its implications for political and economic structures. Such proclamation is and will be costly. The conflict and chaos and sheer influence of the dominating empire may tempt us to passivity, fear, cynicism, even despair.

So, like Jesus, we need to be attentive to and grateful for *Abba* God's faithful and liberating love, experienced especially in the life shared by people. Like Luke's community, we need to hear words of comfort, promise, and hope—but also of challenge.

One final example. For their final exam in one of my theology courses, I asked my students to explain and discuss the relationship of three quotations. Archbishop Helder Camara of Brazil: "When I fed the poor, they called me a saint. When I asked, 'Why are they poor?' They called me a Communist." John Kavanaugh, S.J.: "Christianity at rock bottom radically conflicts with American culture, even subverts it." Pope John Paul II: "The pillars of true peace are justice and that form of love which is forgiveness."

One of the students wrote: "Some Americans are more loyal to the values of capitalism and nationalism than they are to their religious roots. I know this because I was one of them. In high school, I would have labeled myself as a right wing conservative. After all, I opposed abortion, believed in a strong work ethic, supported the war against terrorism (after all, they were evil), and hard core supported Wal-Mart (after all, it *is* capitalism).... I believed I was a 'true American.' But now, I wonder if I was really a 'true hypocrite.' While upholding my beliefs in capitalism and nationalism, did I abandon my Christian values?"

She goes on to describe her questioning whether her lived values (absorbed, no doubt, from family and advertising and other media) fit Jesus' teachings. In the quotations she recognized "some of the hardest teachings for Americans to put into practice." More important, the exam gave her the opportunity to examine carefully some values and convictions, and so to find words and insight as she tried to connect her religious values with her socioeconomic values.

This student's struggle is not limited to citizens of the United States. It can face many who consider themselves Christian. Authentic discipleship calls for careful reflection and critical choice. Such examination of our assumptions and convictions is essential for all of us in so many dimensions of our lives. Where in your life is your class or gender or political party more influential than the Gospel?

ENDNOTES

1. Karl Rahner, S.J., *Theological Investigations Vol. XVIII*, translated by Margaret Kohl, New York: Crossroad, 1981, pp. 74-85.
2. Ladislas Orsy, S.J., "A Time to Ponder," *America*, Vol. 196, No. 4, 5 February 2007, p. 14. For a similar insight from the biblical perspective, see Sandra M. Schneiders, *Written That You May Believe*, New York: Crossroad, 1999, pp. 29-32.
3. John Paul II, "Address of His Holiness Pope John Paul II to the Diplomatic Corps," 13 January 2003, http://www.vatican.va.
4. Arthur J. Dewey, *The Word in Time* (revised edition), New Berlin, WI: Liturgical Publications, 1990, p. 201.
5. Ibid.
6. Ibid., p. 202.

CHAPTER 2

Light Over Darkness

The Meaning of Christmas

The shadow of the cross covers our Christmas crib. During Advent and Christmas, we prepare for and then celebrate God's coming into the world. Still, most of us probably do not ask why God became flesh. If we did, our answers would likely sound something like this: "Jesus came to redeem us." Or more strongly: "Jesus came to die for our sins." Such convictions are found in the Scriptures and expressed in our liturgy. The shadow of the cross is present, even if not the center of our attention during these seasons.

There is, however, an alternative view about why God became human, expressed both in the Scriptures and in the Christian tradition. Though less well known, this perspective, which emphasizes God's overflowing love, offers more light than shadow. This article presents some of the key insights of the different perspective and suggests some implications not only for our celebration of Christmas but also for our everyday relationship with God.

The Cross

First, let's return to the shadow of the cross. Because the life, death and resurrection of Jesus make up the foundation of Christianity, the Christian community has long reflected on their significance for our lives. What was the purpose of Jesus' life? Or simply, why Jesus?

The answer most frequently handed on in everyday religion emphasizes redemption. This view returns to the creation story and sees in Adam and Eve's sin a fundamental alienation from God, a separation so profound that God must intervene to overcome it. The Incarnation, the Word becoming flesh, is considered God's action to right this original wrong. Redemption, then, is basically understood as a "buying back."

How did this view develop? Just as we do when we face tragedy, especially innocent suffering, so the early followers of Jesus tried to make sense of his horrible death. They asked: Why? They sought insight from their Jewish practices, such as Temple sacrifices, and from their Scriptures.

Certain rites and passages (the suffering servant in Isaiah, psalms of lament, wisdom literature on the suffering righteous person) seemed to fit the terrible events at the end of Jesus' life and so offered an answer to the 'why' question. Understandably, these powerful images colored the entire story, including the meaning of Jesus' birth and life.

Throughout the centuries, Christian theology and piety have developed these interpretations of Jesus' execution. At times God has even been described as demanding Jesus' suffering and death as a means of atonement—to satisfy and appease an angry God. In many forms of theology, popular piety and religious practice, the purpose of Jesus' life is directly linked to original sin and all human sinfulness. Without sin, there would have been no need for the Incarnation.

Creation for Incarnation

An interpretation that highlights the Incarnation stands beside this dominant view with its emphasis on sin. The alternate view is also expressed in Scripture and tradition. Nevertheless, the emphasis on the Word made flesh has remained something of a "minority report," rarely gaining the same recognition and influence as the atonement view.

What, briefly, is the heart of this alternate interpretation? It holds that the whole purpose of creation is for the Incarnation, God's sharing of life and love in a unique and definitive way. God becoming human is not an afterthought, an event to make up for original sin and human sinfulness. Incarnation is God's first thought, the original design for all creation. The purpose of Jesus' life is the fulfillment of God's eternal longing to become human.

For many of us who have lived a lifetime with the atonement view, it may be hard at first to hear the minority report. Yet it may offer some wonderful surprises for our relationship with God.

From this perspective, God is appreciated with a different emphasis. God is not an angry or vindictive God, demanding the suffering and death of Jesus as a payment for past sin.

God is, instead, a gracious God, sharing divine life and love in creation and in the Incarnation (like parents sharing their love in the life of a new child). Evidently, such a view can dramatically change our image of God, our celebration of Christmas, our day-by-day prayer.

In order to appreciate this emphasis more fully, let's take the time and effort to look at several of its most important expressions in Scripture and tradition. This brief review will also remind us that the focus on the Incarnation is not just a new fad or some recent "feel good" theology. Its roots go back to the very beginning of Christianity.

He Pitched His Tent Among Us

"In the beginning was the Word, and the Word was with God, and the Word was God....All things came to be through him, and without him nothing came to be....And the Word became flesh...." The Prologue of John's Gospel (1:1-18) gives us this magnificent vision, proclaiming that all creation came to be in the Word, God's self-expression who became flesh, Jesus.

John's meditation on God's supreme act of love in the Incarnation (also see 3:16) has led some theologians to consider that this event alone was sufficient to save the world. Indeed, John's Gospel does not see Jesus' death as a ransom (unlike the synoptic Gospels, for example, Mark 10:45), nor does it use the language of sacrifice or atonement. There is, instead, emphasis on friendship, intimacy, mutuality, service, faithful love — revealing God's desire and gift for the full flourishing of humanity, or in other words, salvation (see the Farewell Address, John 13:1 – 17:26).

Jesus' crucifixion (usually described as being "lifted up") is part of his "hour" of glorification, which also includes his resurrection and ascension. For John, this hour is not sacrifice but epiphany, the manifestation of God.

We may impose sacrificial imagery on John's Gospel because in our hearts and minds we blend together the four Gospels, even though they give us very different portraits of Jesus. If we pay attention to John's emphasis on the Incarnation and on the truth of God revealed in Jesus, we discover part of the foundation of our alternate answer to "Why Jesus?" For John, what is at the heart of reality is a God who wants to share divine life.

A Plan for the Fullness of Time

Another part of the foundation comes from the Letters to the Colossians and the Ephesians. These two letters, written in the tradition of Paul in the latter part of the first century, also offer a cosmic vision from the beginning of time to final fulfillment. They express remarkable beliefs: that Christ is the image of the invisible God, that God chose believers before the foundation of the world, that the goal of God's plan was the coming of Christ, that all things not only find their origin in Christ but are now held together in him and will be fulfilled in God through Christ.

Like John's Prologue, the Letters to the Colossians and the Ephesians connect with and express the Jewish wisdom tradition (see, for example, Proverbs 8, Wisdom 7 and 9). Wisdom was present with God from the beginning; everything was created in and through Wisdom. Unlike John's Gospel, these two Letters include Paul's theology of the cross with its imagery of ransom and sacrifice.

Ephesians and Colossians offer a magnificent vision of God's plan and initiative, revealed and fulfilled in Christ. This plan of salvation, an expression of God's wisdom, is eternal and not just an afterthought to sin. The letters acknowledge sin and sacrifice, but emphasize God's overflowing love from before creation until final fulfillment of the universe.

A Dance of Love

Throughout the centuries, the Christian community has carried on a dialogue with the Scriptures and the community's experience, always searching for understanding and appropriate ways to express its beliefs. Naturally, individual theologians and Church Councils made use of the philosophies and other insights of their age.

During the first centuries of Christianity's existence, questions about Jesus and the Trinity raised special interest. How can we speak of this human being who is also God? How can we speak of one God who is Father, Son, and Spirit? (What many of us now simply accept as part of our Creed had to be hammered out over many years.)

Three people who played a very important role in that process during the fourth century were St. Basil of Caesarea, St. Gregory of Nyssa and St. Gregory of Nazianzus. Because they lived in Cappadocia (an area of present-day Turkey), these three saints are simply called the Cappadocians. For many of us in the West, their thought is not well known.

A key concept in their teaching about how the Trinity is both one and three is *perichoresis*, a term conveying dynamic and creative energy, eternal movement, mutuality and interrelatedness. The three divine persons are what they are by relation to one another. Some scholars like to use the image of dance to describe this term. In this divine dance there is an eternal movement of reciprocal giving and receiving, expressing the essence and unity of God. Moreover, this interrelatedness of the triune God is not self-contained but is poured out in creation, Incarnation and final fulfillment. God is overflowing love, leading humanity and all creation into the divine dance of God's life.

A Franciscan View

Hundreds of years later, in the Middle Ages, the question about Jesus was expressed very explicitly: Would the Son of God have become incarnate if humanity had not sinned? The great theologian St. Thomas Aquinas (1225-1274) answered in the negative, viewing the Incarnation as a remedy for sin.

Another great philosopher and theologian, Franciscan John Duns Scotus (1266-1308), disagreed with Thomas's emphasis on sin. Indeed, Duns Scotus boldly proclaimed and defended the primacy of the Incarnation. He based his view on the Scriptures, early theologians, and logic. He argued, for example, that God's supreme work, the Incarnation, had to be first and foremost in God's mind. It could not be dependent on or occasioned by any action of humans, especially sin.

Even more than logic, Duns Scotus emphasized divine love. God is love and created all life in order to communicate to creatures the fullness of divine love. The Incarnate Word is the foundation of the creative plan of God, the very reason for the existence of all creation. This emphasis on Christ as the center and cornerstone of all creation has become an essential dimension of Franciscan life and ministry.

Alpha and Omega

New and different questions emerged in the 20th century. Jesuit scientist Pierre Teilhard de Chardin confronted the reality of evolution and realized the need for a new way to speak of the mystery of God.

As a paleontologist, Teilhard studied fossils and other clues of our ancient past. As a believer, he returned to the foundations in Colossians and Ephesians and built on the long tradition that proclaimed Christ as the reason for the entire order of creation. He saw Christ as the Alpha, the very beginning of the evolutionary process, in whom all things were created (COL 1:15).

Teilhard especially looked to the future. From the scientific perspective, he saw that there had to be a point which governs the whole of evolution, a power of attraction which provides evolution's intrinsic drive and orientation. From the faith perspective, he saw that the glorified Christ is the Omega, the final point in whom all things will be gathered up (EPH 1:10). Teilhard realized that the two perspectives focused on the same reality: Christ, the very soul of evolution, the Omega point in whom everything will be unified by and in love.

Teilhard struggled to heal the deep tension between science and religion that led so many to turn away from belief in God. He offered to the modern world a positive worldview, uniting evolution and human efforts with the presence and action of Christ, all the while acknowledging the dark reality of evil.

God's Self-communication

The twentieth century continued to raise serious questions and challenges to faith and religion. Numerous wars and other horrors led to pessimism and cynicism, doubt and denial. Relying on his extensive knowledge of the Christian tradition and of contemporary philosophies, Jesuit theologian Karl Rahner (1904-1984) developed a profound response to these questions and challenges.

Rahner always stressed that God is a holy and incomprehensible mystery. We have come to know the Trinitarian God (but never fully) in and through God's wonderful deeds in the world and in history. The very heart of this revelation, Rahner proclaimed, is God's self-communication: God's overflowing love leading to Jesus and so first to creation and grace and ultimately to beatific vision. God's free decision to communicate divine life can be viewed as the reason for the world.

God's self-communication also occurs in the depths of our being. Rahner understood the human person as spirit in the world, a finite being with an infinite capacity. If we are to satisfy our deepest human yearnings, we need grace. For Rahner, grace is God's self-gift, God's personal fulfillment of our natural openness, offered freely to all persons, transforming the core of human life.

Like Teilhard, Rahner affirmed the presence of God in the whole world. All human experience offers the possibility of encounter with God. God's love is also the real basis of the world's hope. God's self-communication as beatific vision will be the final fulfillment of all history and peoples. Then, indeed, God will be "all in all" (1 COR 15:28).

What Difference Does It Make?

For almost 2,000 years, believers have found hope and light in recognizing the primacy of the Incarnation. God's overflowing love wants to embody itself in and for others. Jesus is the first thought, not an afterthought. Does this remarkable belief make any difference in our lives? Absolutely, especially for those of us whose faith has been shaped by images of atonement and expiation.

First, the perspective of creation-for-Incarnation highlights the rich meaning of Jesus. He is not Plan B, sent simply to make up for sin. As Duns Scotus emphasized so well, God's masterpiece must result from something much greater and more positive (God's desire to share life and love).

If some shadow of the cross remains over the crib, it comes from the fact of Jesus' execution, a fact that does not express the full meaning and purpose of his life. There is more light than shadow: Jesus is the culmination of God's self-gift to the world.

Second, the focus on the Word made flesh helps us to appreciate the depth of our humanness and the importance of our actions. Rahner's marvelous musings on our life in a world of grace give us renewed understanding of the biblical phrase "created in God's image" — along with many implications for how we treat all our sisters and brothers in the human family. Teilhard's cosmic vision inspires us to see and take our part in the great evolutionary process, in a particular way (along with Francis of Assisi) in our care for the earth.

Third and most important, our "minority report" offers a new and transformed image of God. Many people suspect that the dominant perspective of God demanding the suffering and death of the Son as atonement somehow missed the mark.

Indeed, Rahner gently says that the idea of a sacrifice of blood offered to God may have been current at the time of Jesus, but is of little help today. Rahner offers other interpretations of how Jesus saves us, emphasizing that God's saving will for all people was fully realized in Jesus through the perfect response of his whole life.

Other contemporary scholars, including Walter Wink, are more direct. He states that the early disciples simply were unable to sustain Jesus' vision of the compassionate and nonviolent reign of God. Overwhelmed by Jesus' horrible death and searching for some meaning, the disciples slipped back into an older religious conviction that believed violence (sacrifice) saves.

The emphasis on Jesus as the first thought can free us from those images and allow us to focus on God's overflowing love. This love is the very life of the Trinity and spills over into creation, grace, Incarnation and final flourishing and fulfillment.

What a difference this makes for our relationship with God! We are invited into this divine dance. Life and love, not suffering and death, become the core of our spirituality and our morality. Our prayer—and every celebration of Advent and Christmas—allows our spirits to soar in the light rather than crouch in the shadow.

"In the beginning was the Word...and the Word became flesh." *Alleluia!*

CHAPTER 3

Finding the Heart of Jesus' Life

How do you and I learn to be Christian disciples if not by exploring the events of Jesus' life? We can discover Jesus' experience only by listening carefully to what the Christian community said about him in the Scriptures. Yet the Scriptures, as the Church teaches, are accounts of faith rooted in history. Thus Scripture writers were not so much concerned with historical details as they were with conveying the meaning of Jesus' presence among us. How do we get to the Jesus that the disciples encountered, the experiences behind the statements of faith?

Because Scripture and Church teachings emphasize the divinity of Jesus, our own experience of Jesus is just about the opposite from the disciples' experience of him. The disciples first encountered someone they knew as a fellow human being, Jesus of Nazareth. Only gradually — indeed, not clearly until after the Resurrection — would they recognize and proclaim his divinity (see "The Historical Truth of the Gospels," the 1964 *Instruction* of the Roman Pontifical Biblical Commission).

For those of us who come almost 2,000 years later, faith in Jesus' divinity is almost taken for granted, for it is affirmed throughout the gospels. Indeed, many of us may find it easier to believe that Jesus is God than to accept that he was truly human. In order to appreciate as fully as possible the events in the life of Jesus of Nazareth, we must follow the same path that the disciples followed, beginning with the human Jesus. In this chapter, we'll look at Jesus' vision and his encounters with others as found in the gospels. In doing so, we'll get a glimpse at the heart of his earthly life.

Jesus' Birth

Only two New Testament books describe the birth of Jesus: Luke (1:1–2:52) and Matt (1:1–2:23). But the two stories are very, very different in their details. Because most of us have combined the two stories in our hearts and minds, we realize these differences only by looking at the two accounts separately. Matthew focuses on Joseph, has Mary and Joseph living in Bethlehem, and includes the Magi and the flight into Egypt. Luke focuses on Mary, has Mary and Joseph living in Nazareth (going to Bethlehem only for the Roman census), and includes the shepherds and a peaceful visit of the Holy Family to Jerusalem.

In his extensive study of the infancy narratives, the late Scripture scholar Raymond Brown emphasizes that what is important is the religious message of the stories. What is this message? Brown claims it is two-fold: to proclaim the identity of Jesus as truly God and truly human and to show how Jesus is linked to and fulfills the Hebrew Scriptures. Brown states that each infancy narrative is, in fact, the whole gospel in miniature: The full identity of Jesus (divine and human) is revealed; this good news is shared with others and accepted by some (shepherds, Magi, Simeon, Anna) but rejected by others (Herod the king, the chief priests and scribes). Accordingly, we must focus on the meaning and not on the details of the stories.

Surely an important dimension of Jesus' life was his experience of religion. The story of the people of Israel was Jesus' story. As he grew, Jesus listened to and prayed with the Hebrew Scriptures. He pondered the lives of Abraham and Moses, of Jeremiah and Isaiah. Their God was Jesus' God—a God who continued to be active in the people's lives, freeing and choosing and calling them back to the covenant. This Jewish context, then, nurtured Jesus' knowledge of and relationship with God.

Jesus' Mission

Luke develops the picture of Jesus' identity and mission in the marvelous and powerful scene of the keynote address in Nazareth (4:14-30). Scripture scholars help us to appreciate Luke's creativity as artist and as theologian. Writing his gospel many years after the death and resurrection of Jesus, Luke wanted to share his community's experience and commitment and vision. So he felt free to rearrange his primary source, Mark's Gospel, by moving this Nazareth synagogue scene (MARK 6:1FF) to the very beginning of Jesus' public ministry (LUKE 4:14FF). Luke's creativity is also found within the text itself, as he weaves together selections from several different chapters of Isaiah and omits some other points.

As it stands, the exact text that Luke puts on Jesus' lips would not be found on a synagogue scroll. This passage is truly a keynote, establishing the basic themes of Luke's Gospel. Jesus, the anointed one (the Messiah, the Christ), teaches and heals and proclaims the presence of God's reign. Jesus is the fulfillment of God's promises for the hungry, the sick, the imprisoned. The following chapter is an elaboration on this concept of Jesus' keynote address.

Indeed, Luke's Gospel goes on to describe many examples of Jesus teaching and healing the poor, including Peter's mother-in-law and the leper. Then, when some disciples of John the Baptist ask Jesus, "Are you the one who is to come?" Jesus replies: "Go and tell John what you have seen and heard: The blind regain their sight, the lame walk, lepers are cleansed, the deaf hear, the dead are raised, the poor have the good news proclaimed to them" (LUKE 7:20-22). God's reign is breaking into the world through Jesus.

Jesus' Relationship with God

In attempting to appreciate the heart of Jesus' life, as we have already seen, we must pay special attention to Jesus' faithful and loving relationship with God and to Jesus' understanding of the reign of God.

Scripture scholars have helped us to appreciate the significance of Jesus' relationship with God, whom he addressed as "Father" and even "*Abba*." Some scholars say that Jesus chose this word that small children used to address their fathers. *Abba* is best translated "Daddy." It conveys a sense of childlike simplicity and familiarity.

Other Scripture scholars have recently offered the image of patron for understanding Jesus' use of *Father*. Appreciating the cultural world of the first century suggests this alternative interpretation, which implies a mature personal relationship with the one who empowers and distributes benefits, emphasizing trust, responsibility, and fidelity.

Although offering different emphases, these images are important for our consideration of Jesus' experience because they point to a very profound relationship between God and Jesus.

How did it develop? We have no way of answering in detail, but we can assume that this bond developed gradually as Jesus lived life, heard the Hebrew Scriptures, asked himself about his own response to God, listened to John the Baptist, and began his own prophetic ministry, taking time to be alone and to pray. The God of Jacob, Deborah, Hannah, David, Amos, Ezekiel was Father to Jesus.

We catch another glimpse into Jesus' experience of God in the parables. One of the most helpful is Luke 15:11-32 — traditionally called the parable of the Prodigal Son. This parable about the possibility of reconciliation is better described, however, as the parable of the Forgiving Father. The details are familiar: The younger son demands his inheritance, leaves home, spends all the money, and finally returns to his father's house, asking to be treated as a servant.

Notice the actions of the father: he allows his son freedom even to waste the inheritance; he watches for his return. He forgives the son without any bitterness. Throwing a party to celebrate, he goes out to console the angry older brother.

In this parable, Jesus is telling us a lot about his own experience of God. Abba is both a dispenser of goods and a forgiving, gentle parent. Jesus evidently feels very close to this personal God, a God who reaches out to all, both those who wander away and those who stay at home.

Jesus' Focus on the Reign of God

If we look closely at the events and teachings of Jesus' life, we see that Jesus focused his energies neither on himself nor on the Church. Jesus' whole life was directed to the reign of God, a central image in the gospels. Simply put, the reign means that God's power is at work in a particular situation. God's saving presence is found there. The reign (also called kingdom or sovereignty in some translations) does not imply a particular place or time; the reign is present whenever and wherever God's loving presence is manifested. Therefore the reign may exist in individual persons, in institutions, and in the whole world. The miracles of Jesus are symbols of God's reign breaking into our world, of healing and salvation overcoming brokenness and sin.

Let's look at one powerful example given in the gospels. For the people of Israel, leprosy had become not only a medical problem but also a ritual impurity. The people considered the disease to be divine punishment and feared that the community would also suffer if the leper were not forced outside the town.

Jesus not only rejects the judgment but also crosses the boundaries of purity laws to touch the alienated. Mark's Gospel describes the scene this way: "A leper came to him [and kneeling down] begged him and said, 'If you wish, you can make me clean.' Moved with pity, he stretched out his hand, touched him, and said to him, 'I do will it. Be made clean.' The leprosy left him immediately, and he was made clean" (1:40-42).

With a simple but profound touch, Jesus breaks down barriers, challenges customs and laws that alienate, and embodies his convictions about the inclusive meaning of the reign of God. This dramatic touch is also described in Matt 8:1-4 and Luke 5:12-16.

This event reveals not only Jesus' care for an individual in need but also his concern about structures of society. Jesus steps across the boundaries separating the unclean and actually touches the leper. In doing so, Jesus enters into the leper's isolation and becomes unclean. Human care and compassion, not cultural values of honor and shame, direct Jesus' action. He calls into question the purity code, which alienates and oppresses people already in need. Indeed, this encounter with the leper is one example of how Jesus reaches out to the marginal people in Jewish society, whether they be women, the possessed, or lepers.

Teaching God's Reign by Parable

Jesus used parables to speak about the kingdom, or reign of God. Although he thus risked being misunderstood, Jesus allowed his listeners to make the connection between what he was talking about and what they were already expecting. He usually upset many of their preconceived notions of God's righteousness and power. Yet he took a chance that his words would touch the people in their depths and that they would act upon this discovery. He did so because he believed that the reign of God, so evident in his own experience, could — and would — be recognized by others.

At times, Jesus began his parables with the statement, "The Kingdom of God is like...." At other times, this statement is only implied. In Luke 8:4-15, for instance, Jesus simply begins, "A sower went out to sow his seed," and goes on to describe the different types of ground on which the seed fell. Part of *our* need in hearing this parable is to recognize that Jesus is describing very poor farming techniques. His hearers at the time, of course, knew that; they also knew that even the best techniques of the day produced about sevenfold. But in the parable, the rich soil produces a hundredfold. Jesus is telling his listeners how surprising God's reign is, how overflowing in goodness — not sevenfold but a hundredfold!

A similar parable can also be misunderstood because we do not know specifics from Jesus' day. In Luke 13:20-21, Jesus describes a woman mixing yeast into three measures of flour. Most of us miss the heart of Jesus' teaching because we do not know that three "measures" of flour is enough for fifty pounds of bread!

Years ago in an *I Love Lucy* TV episode, Lucy was baking bread and this huge loaf just kept rising and coming out of the oven, finally pinning her against the kitchen wall. The exaggeration of the Lucy show expresses the heart of the parable. The kingdom of God is full of joy and surprise and goodness.

Because of Jesus' intimate relationship with God, Jesus experienced the presence of the reign in and through his own life. And what he tried to tell others in his parables is that they could experience this reign too!

Jesus' Sermon on the Mount

Another section of the gospels which provides rich insight into Jesus' experience of God's loving and saving presence is what we commonly know as the Sermon on the Mount (although the location in Luke's Gospel is level ground — see Luke 6:17-49; see also Matt 5:1 – 7:29). In this collection of Jesus' teachings, we discover some of the surprise and goodness of the reign: the hungry will be satisfied; those who weep now will laugh; those who are poor will be part of God's kingdom.

The Sermon also gives other characteristics of life in the reign: love of enemies, generosity, compassion, forgiveness, humility, and nonviolence. Especially here we confront the challenge expressed in Jesus' understanding of God's kingdom. "Love your enemies, do good to those who hate you, bless those who curse you, pray for those who mistreat you" (Luke 6:27-28). "Be merciful, just as your Father is merciful" (Luke 6:36). And, as is typical of Luke's Gospel, we also hear about the dangers of wealth and complacency (Luke 6:24-26).

Death and Resurrection

Let's now look at the end of Jesus' life: his passion, death, and resurrection. As with the infancy accounts, we tend to combine the different passion narratives in our hearts and minds. Still, there are significant differences in the four portraits. For example, Mark describes Jesus as abandoned by his disciples, rejected by the crowd, and seemingly forsaken by his God.

But John describes Jesus as being in control, freely laying down his life, and dying in a sovereign and life-giving manner. In his portrait of the passion, Luke continues to emphasize the same characteristics and experiences of Jesus found throughout the gospel: compassion and healing, forgiveness and profound trust. Thus even the passion accounts, while rooted in a historical fact (the Crucifixion), are stories of faith in which theology, not biography, determines how events are narrated.

But the passion and death are only the beginning of Jesus' glorification. The Resurrection completes this central event. In the descriptions of the Resurrection, we find much symbolic language: dazzling lights, appearances sudden as a flash, a mysterious inability to recognize Jesus but then ecstatic joy with the recognition, a sudden fading away. All this reminds us that the Resurrection is a different kind of reality, not the same kind of historical event as the Crucifixion.

The Resurrection is an experience in faith, known and proclaimed by the disciples yet denied by unbelievers. The Resurrection can be understood as God's affirmation of Jesus' faithfulness and trust. Abba's power raises Jesus to transformed life. The disciples experience Jesus as alive in a new way. His presence transforms them and their world.

At the heart of Jesus' living and dying are his intimate, loving relationship with God and his bold, creative proclamation of God's reign. We twenty-first-century disciples of Jesus are called to live and share this good news!

CHAPTER 4

Jesus' Keynote Address

Glad Tidings of Healing and Hope

What better direction for our life and ministry can there be than Jesus' own keynote address! This marvelous and powerful scene in the gospel of Luke (4:14-21) is rich with statements about Jesus' identity and mission, and full of implications for our lives as disciples of Jesus. Let's take some time to pay attention to this passage, which presents the gospel in miniature.

Scripture scholars help us to appreciate Luke's creativity as artist and as theologian. Writing his gospel many years after the death and resurrection of Jesus, Luke, of course, was not intending an exact historical account but rather a proclamation of faith. He wanted to share his community's experience and commitment and vision. So he felt free to rearrange his primary source, Mark's gospel, by moving this scene to the very beginning of Jesus' public ministry. Luke's creativity is also found within the text itself, as he weaves together selections from several different chapters of Isaiah and omits some other points. As it stands, this text would not be found on a synagogue scroll. Luke acts as artist in order to be preacher.

This passage is truly a keynote, establishing the basic themes of Luke's gospel. Jesus, the anointed one (Hebrew: *Messiah*; Greek: *Christ*), teaches and heals and proclaims the presence of God's reign. Jesus is the fulfillment of God's promises for the hungry, the sick, the imprisoned.

Indeed, Luke's gospel goes on to describe many examples of Jesus teaching and healing the poor, including both Peter's mother–in–law and a leper. Then, when some disciples of John the Baptist ask Jesus, "Are you the one who is to come," Jesus replies: "Go and tell John what you have seen and heard: the blind receive their sight, the lame walk, the lepers are cleansed, the deaf hear, the dead are raised, the poor have good news brought to them" (LUKE 7:20-23). God's reign is breaking into the world through Jesus.

And it continues to happen today—through us. As Luke was creative with Mark and Isaiah, let us be creative with Luke: "The Spirit of the Lord is upon us, because the Spirit has anointed us to bring good news to the poor. The Spirit has sent us to proclaim release to the captives and recovery of sight to the blind, to let the oppressed go free, to proclaim the year of the Lord's favor. . . . Today this scripture is being fulfilled in our hearing."

Amazing, isn't it? And absolutely true! We have been anointed by the Spirit in our baptism. We have been deeply loved by our gentle God, experiencing God's favor in so many ways. We have been sent out to proclaim glad tidings.

It is essential for us to remember and celebrate our identity, rooted in the life and teachings of Jesus. We want to hear again our call to follow him. We want to find renewed courage and wisdom in order to teach and to heal and to free. For that is what we do in our amazing variety of ministries and with our own families and friends and colleagues. And all this in very ordinary ways, with day–to–day details, sometimes with little recognition or appreciation from others.

Luke's text speaks of "the year of the Lord's favor," tapping into those special feelings of the jubilee when people returned to their homes, debts were canceled, and slaves were set free. Even the structures of social and economic life must reflect God's reign. Still we need not wait for the extraordinary time. We live every day in a world of grace. The great theologian, Karl Rahner, has reminded us in one of his prayers of this important insight. Let's listen in:

> "*Every* day is 'everyday.' ... If it's true [O God] that I can lose You in everything, it must also be true that I can find You in everything. If You have given me no single place to which I can flee and be sure of finding You, ... then I must be able to find You in every place, in each and every thing I do. Otherwise I couldn't find You at all, and this cannot be, since I can't possibly exist without You. Thus, I must seek You in all things. If every day is 'everyday,' then every day is Your day, and every hour is the hour of Your grace".[1]

Every year is a year of the Lord's favor. "Today this scripture is being fulfilled in our hearing."

Let's return to Luke's gospel and re-enter the scene of Jesus' keynote address. Almost immediately the scene turns sour as his own people drive Jesus out of town (LUKE 4:21-30). And so Luke introduces other key themes of Jesus' life and ministry: conflict and rejection. The threat here is finally fulfilled in the Crucifixion. Perhaps the mysterious "he passed through their midst" foreshadows the Resurrection.

Along with the rejection by the people of Nazareth comes an essential Lucan theme: universalism. The good news is for all people, not just for Israel in need.

By the time Luke's gospel was written, the story of Jesus had moved beyond the boundaries of Palestine. Indeed, Luke's community existed as a result of this move. We see even more clearly in his second volume, the Acts of the Apostles, that Luke emphasizes the spread of glad tidings to the whole world.

This more sobering part of Luke's keynote scene also speaks to us. As disciples of Jesus we too encounter conflict and rejection. We live in a culture and world marked by individualism, consumerism, and violence of all kinds. Jesus' message and example of healing and gentleness is so desperately needed and yet is consistently rejected by the powers of domination.

We know too that much conflict occurs within the Church itself. Suspicion between liberals and conservatives, bitterness, oppression of groups, suppression of ideas all too often infect the body of Christ. We too are rejected by our own people. So, Jesus' example of faithful ministry, whatever the threat, is especially important. And also, of course, the Resurrection, which grounds our hope.

Relying on God's promise, we desire to share the good news with all the world, starting with our own communities. We desire to follow Jesus in crossing boundaries that separate people. Yet in all this we also acknowledge our own limits, even sinfulness. We too reject other members of our community. We too get trapped in sexism and racism and classism, and so build barriers between our sisters and brothers, other images of God. We need to turn to another scene in Luke's gospel (15:11-32), the story of the Prodigal Son, and to trust that the forgiving father rushes out to meet us in loving compassion.

Another section of Luke's gospel, the Sermon on the Plain (6:17-49), helps us to appreciate even more the glad tidings we are sent out to proclaim. We hear the heart of what we are to teach; we experience the healing we are to share; we glimpse the kind of life our freedom serves.

If we are honest, we probably have to admit that Jesus' vision surprises us. It just does not make sense. What makes sense is to make lots of money, to have security and power. Jesus says happy are the poor and the hungry. What makes sense is to create tougher laws and build more prisons. Jesus urges people to be merciful and to love their enemies. What makes sense is that we harbor anger and resentment towards a spouse or parent, a stranger or terrorist. Jesus teaches forgiveness and prayer for persecutors.

In so many ways in his life and teachings, Jesus surprises us, turning our expectations upside-down, helping us to appreciate the difference and newness of the reign of God. Still we get trapped in "what makes sense" according to our culture, to common sense, even to some religious custom.

So Jesus' keynote address gives us the opportunity to learn again the meaning of life, to glimpse the very core of God's loving design. It invites us to appreciate ever more deeply both God's amazing love and our vocation to live as faithful disciples of Jesus. It leads us to refocus our attention on who we are and what we do by contemplating the identity and mission of Jesus.

With Jesus, we are called and anointed. With Jesus, we are sent out to teach, to heal, to free. With Jesus, we face conflict and rejection. With Jesus,

we reach out to all with compassion, especially the economically, physically, and socially poor. With Jesus, we proclaim with passion glad tidings
of healing and hope.

ENDNOTE

1. Karl Rahner, *Prayers for a Lifetime*, New York: Crossroad, 1986, pp. 92, 93.

CHAPTER 5

Vatican II

Aggiornamento as Healing

In 1959 Pope John XXIII stunned the world when, after being pope for only 90 days, he announced his plan to convene the Second Vatican Council (only the twenty-first ecumenical council in the life of the Church). Such a dramatic event was not at all expected from the elderly Pope John. Yet he recognized the serious need for renewal in the Church, and so made his call to begin the process of *aggiornamento* ("updating"). Many aspects of life in the Church needed to be brought up to date, and deep divisions needed to be healed. This chapter will describe these divisions and how the council's teachings brought reform and new life.

Earlier Councils

Roman Catholicism in 1959 was still profoundly shaped by an earlier gathering of all the bishops of the Church, the Council of Trent (1545-1563). The sixteenth century was, of course, a time of great upheaval in the Church. It was a time of serious abuses, needed reforms, regional politics, and bitter polemics.

The Council of Trent provided an urgently needed response, one that was very effective in revitalizing the life of the Church. Trent took a firm and clear stance on such issues as justification and the sacraments; it strengthened the role of the pope and bishops and began reforms to improve the education of clergy; it reformed and unified the celebration of the Mass and introduced catechisms for the education of the people.

The Church paid a high price for Trent's rigorous reform, however. The response, while clear, was also very defensive and authoritarian; the polemics did not allow acknowledging the Protestant reformers' valid insights. Trent chose to restructure the Church according to a medieval model: papal supremacy, absolute control of the diocese by the bishop, no lay participation in administration. The council also failed to restore people's participation in the Mass; Latin was continued and the vernacular prohibited (one of Luther's reforms was to translate the Bible into the language of the people).

Trent brought renewal to many areas of Church life: spiritual, intellectual, cultural and missionary. But, because of the negative elements, the reform of Trent gradually slipped into a rigid religion. More and more, Roman Catholicism reacted defensively to the growth of the modern world. The next ecumenical council, Vatican I (1869-1870), reinforced these authoritarian and reactionary elements.[1]

The Spirit of Saint John XXIII

What was energizing and renewing in the 1500s had become oppressive by the 1900s. So John XXIII opened the windows for some fresh air. His opening address to Vatican II set the tone for the council, calling not for condemnations but for patience and openness, acknowledging not only the errors but also the opportunities of the time, disagreeing with the prophets of gloom and offering an optimistic and pastoral view of the Church and the world. John affirmed that with Christ there is goodness, order, and peace. The fundamental concern for the council, therefore, became the effective proclamation of the Christian truth for the twentieth century. John stressed both authentic faithfulness to the tradition (*ressourcement* — a return to the sources — was another important dynamic in the council) and the need to find appropriate expressions of that tradition in the modern world.[2]

With remarkable dedication and sometimes intense disagreement the council responded to John's challenge! Meeting in four sessions between 1962 and 1965, Vatican II produced sixteen documents and a renewed vision of Roman Catholicism. One way to view this renewal and reform is to consider three major divisions which the council began to heal: the division within Roman Catholicism itself, the division between Roman Catholicism and other religions (both Christian and non-Christian), and the division between Roman Catholicism and the world.

Healing Within the Church

Vatican II both reflected and addressed the differences within the Church. Although there is an uneven quality to the documents, three deserve attention here: the documents on revelation, liturgy and — most important — the Dogmatic Constitution on the Church (*Lumen Gentium*).

The development of the Dogmatic Constitution on Divine Revelation (*Dei Verbum*) demonstrates well the progressive mentality of Vatican II. The original draft, written by a pre-council commission, emphasized traditional formulas in a defensive and negative tone. After spirited debate, the document was rejected by a majority of the council members and returned by John XXIII to a new commission for complete rewriting.[3] This newer work made use of a 1964 *Instruction* of the Roman Pontifical Biblical Commission, "The Historical Truth of the Gospels." The *Instruction* stresses that attention be paid to the three stages that are part of the process of the formation of the gospels: "(1) the ministry of Jesus, (2) the preaching of the apostles and (3) the writing by the evangelists."[4]

The new version of the Constitution on Divine Revelation then, finally approved in the last session of the council, relied on modern biblical and historical research. The document emphasizes that revelation is God's gracious self-manifestation. Saying yes to this personal encounter with God is faith. This experience is handed on orally (Tradition) and in writing (Scripture). Both Scripture and Tradition, of course, must be handed on by a living community that preserves and re-expresses their meaning, applying them to new situations. The renewed understanding of the Bible, along with the emphasis on it in this document on revelation, provides the basis for the inner renewal of the whole Church.

The document that probably had the most immediate and visible impact on the Church was the Constitution on the Sacred Liturgy (*Sacrosanctum Concilium*). This document, based on the vast research and scholarship of the liturgical pioneers, led to the major revision of the Mass. Worship no longer would appear to be just the action of a priest, back turned to the people, speaking in a language most did not understand. The reformed liturgy would focus on community worship: the participation of the people, use of the vernacular, renewed emphasis on Scripture. "In the restoration and development of the sacred liturgy the full and active participation by all the people is the paramount concern, for it is the primary, indeed the *indispensable* source from which the faithful are to derive the true Christian spirit."[5] Although not all the changes were introduced as well as they might have been, the renewal of the liturgy began to heal the split between clergy and laity in the most important religious experience of everyday Christian living.

The significance of the Dogmatic Constitution on the Church cannot be stressed enough. "Vatican II was a council of the church, for the church and about the church. And nowhere is the church's own self-understanding — its sense of itself, its nature and its purpose — laid out as clearly as in *Lumen Gentium*."[6] Like the document on revelation this document was also drastically revised. Again, a first draft was rejected, and followed by a new document that was more biblical, historical and dynamic. By re-imaging the Church as the "people of God," this final version radically changed the Church's self-understanding. It marked the beginning of the healing of deep divisions within the Church.

One of these divisions was another kind of separation between clergy and laity. The document on the Church stressed the dignity and responsibilities of the laity and set aside the purely hierarchical point of view. Authority was now to be viewed in terms of service. An entire chapter of the document is devoted to the laity. But even more important, its basic image of the Church as the "new people of God" clearly emphasizes the human and communal nature of the Church rather than the institutional and hierarchical dimensions. Indeed, it stresses the fundamental equality of all in terms of vocation, dignity and commitment.

A second division within the Church was between bishops and pope. Vatican I had just completed its work on the papacy when Rome was invaded, precipitating a hasty and premature conclusion to the Council. It ended, therefore, without being able to discuss the rest of the Church. In Vatican II's document on the Church, especially with its discussion of collegiality, that earlier council was now balanced.

Vatican II states that all the bishops make up a stable body of people (a "college") that is collectively responsible for the entire Church. The pope acts as head of this college, that is, the supreme authority in the Church is all the bishops together with and under the pope.[7] This union of the primacy of the pope and the authority of the episcopal college begins a new and sometimes tension-filled era in the understanding of Church authority.[8]

Healing Between Catholicism and Other Religions

The second major division that Vatican II addressed was the division between the Roman Catholic Church and other religions (both Christian and non-Christian). The Constitution on the Church takes very seriously ecumenical tensions and opportunities and provides the foundation for dialogue that continues in more detail in several documents, including those on ecumenism, non-Christian religions, and religious freedom.

In the decree on ecumenism (*Unitatis Redintegratio*), Vatican II significantly changes the Church's position relative to non-Catholic Christian communities. It treats them with respect and tries to understand and present their positions fairly. It states that the Spirit is at work in these communities, that they are part of the mystery of salvation.

> Moreover, some, even very many, of the most significant elements and endowments which together go to build up and give life to the church itself, can exist outside the visible boundaries of the Catholic Church: the written Word of God; the life of grace; faith, hope and charity, with the other interior gifts of the Holy Spirit, as well as visible elements.[9]

An important implication here is Vatican II's acknowledgment that Christianity is not limited to Roman Catholicism.

Although brief, the declaration on the relationship of the Church to non-Christian religions (*Nostra Aetate*) expresses a remarkable change, now highlighting the positive contributions and qualities of Hinduism, Islam, Buddhism, and Judaism (which receives special attention). Other religions are included in a more general way. The Council declares that the "Church rejects nothing of what is true and holy in these religions."[10] The declaration ends with a strong rejection of all forms of discrimination or harassment based on race or religion.

Another dramatic breakthrough occurs in the declaration on religious liberty (*Dignitatis Humanae*). The classical Catholic position, as expressed in the 1864 *Syllabus of Errors*, at best tolerated other religions and claimed preferential treatment for the Catholic Church by governments. The religious freedom that is now taken for granted in many countries had not been supported by the Roman Catholic tradition. Historically, numerous countries, including those in Europe, have seen many bloody persecutions related to religious liberty.[11]

Vatican II's document stresses the ethical foundations of the right to religious freedom. "The council further declares that the right to religious freedom is based on the very dignity of the human person as known through the revealed word of God and by reason itself."[12] While the document emphasizes the responsibility to search for truth, especially religious truth, it insists that each person must be free from coercion, especially in religious matters. No one can be forced to act in a way that is contrary to personal beliefs; no one can be forcibly restrained from acting in accordance with those beliefs as long as the just requirements of the common good are observed.

This declaration, not surprisingly, generated much controversy. The issue was not only religious freedom but also the underlying issue of the development of doctrine.[13] The council was concerned about radically changing the position of the Church on religious liberty, a position that had been firmly stated by Pope Pius IX. In the final session of the council, the document was approved by an overwhelming majority.

Healing Between Church and World

The third major division addressed by Vatican II was the separation of the Church from the world. Discussed in many documents, this topic was the specific focus of the Pastoral Constitution on the Church in the Modern World (*Gaudium et Spes*). This significant document clearly expresses and symbolizes the spirit of Vatican II, for it is the only document to have originated directly from a suggestion (by Cardinal Suenens) made during the council itself. With it Vatican II begins a realistic dialogue with the external world. The council accepts the progressive cultural and social movements of modern history and, grounded in its faith, optimistically describes the building of the human community.

This long document is divided into two parts. The first spells out a religious anthropology that is the foundation of many conciliar, papal, and episcopal documents. Included in this description are discussions of the dignity of the person, the interdependence of persons and societies, the significance of human activity in the world, and the role of the Church in the modern world. The second part applies this Christian understanding of the person in community to some of the most critical problems of the contemporary world: marriage and family, the proper development of culture, economic and social and political life, and war and peace. The most distinctive note sounded throughout this progressive and optimistic text is that of the Church putting itself consciously at the service of the human family, as expressed in the now famous opening lines: "The joys and hopes, the grief and anguish of the people of our time, especially of those who are poor or afflicted, are the joys and hopes, the grief and anguish of the followers of Christ as well."[14]

The separation of the Church from the world is overcome in yet another way — in the Church's own self-understanding. That is, Vatican II marks the beginning of the Church understanding itself from a global perspective. Karl Rahner SJ (who was very involved in the council) compares the significance of this breakthrough to the opening of the early Christian community to the Gentiles more than 1,900 years ago. Rahner uses the image of "world-Church" to describe this new self-understanding.[15] By world-Church Rahner means that Roman Catholicism is no longer a European and Western religion that has been "exported" to the rest of the world. It has now allowed itself truly to be shaped by a whole variety of cultures from Latin America, Asia, and Africa.

Past and Present

Vatican II stands as a remarkable example of renewal and reform. With its emphasis on the Bible, the council turned again to the foundation of the Christian experience and found renewed means of expressing that experience in the modern world. Deep divisions within the Church began to be healed; aloofness and separation from other religions and the world itself were seriously addressed. Scholars, some of whom had been questioned or silenced in pre-council days, first prepared the way by their scholarship and then actively worked with the bishops at the council to help create a new vision of the Church. Vatican II carefully considered the signs of the times and responded by moving Roman Catholicism beyond its siege mentality to become an open and pastoral community in the world.

Just as with individuals, however, diseases and divisions also re-emerge in the people of God. The years immediately following the close of the council were marked by a wide variety of responses, including bitter debates about appropriate liturgical celebrations and about structures of authority. "Thanks to the Second Vatican Council, Catholics [were] forced to re-examine many of their most cherished practices and traditions. Such a process was bound to be disruptive, but the sheer magnitude of the crisis it provoked astonished everyone."[16]

In recent years as polarization increased in the Church, the debate about the proper interpretation of Vatican II intensified. In his article "Misdirections"[17] Vatican II scholar John O'Malley SJ addresses some of these controversies concerning issues that "should be of concern to all Catholics who cherish the heritage of the council."[18] In pointing out how not to interpret Vatican II, O'Malley clearly also makes positive points.

Several of these points address the interpretations that downplay the significance of the Second Vatican Council. O'Malley stresses that Vatican II was a doctrinal council as well as a pastoral one. It taught many things though "in a style different from previous councils."[19] He emphasizes that significant change happened in the council. Similarly he affirms continuity but also discontinuity in its teachings; the healing expressed in both collegiality and religious liberty are examples of such change.[20]

Given the examples of healing and the need for new healing, the purpose and inspiration of Vatican II, expressed in the council's Opening Message to Humanity, still offers sound direction for all Christians today: "under the guidance of the Holy Spirit, we wish to inquire how we ought to renew ourselves, so that we may be found increasingly faithful to the gospel of Christ."[21]

ENDNOTES

1. Thomas Bokenkotter, *A Concise History of the Catholic Church*, revised and expanded edition (New York: Doubleday, 1990), 214-228, 276-294.

2. Pope John's Opening Speech to the Council, *The Documents of Vatican II*, edited by Walter M. Abbott SJ (New York: The America Press, 1966), 710-719.

3. John W. O'Malley, *What Happened at Vatican II* (Cambridge: Harvard University Press, 2008), 5-8 and passim.

4. Raymond Brown SS, *Reading the Gospels with the Church* (Eugene, Ore.: Wipf and Stock, 2008), 10. This book's first two chapters offer excellent insights—in a very readable fashion—into the interpretation and adaptation contained in the gospels.

5. Constitution on the Sacred Liturgy, *Vatican Council II: The Basic Sixteen Documents*, edited by Austin Flannery OP (Northport, NY: Costello, 1996), §14.

6. Edward P. Hahnenberg, *A Concise Guide to the Documents of Vatican II* (Cincinnati: St. Anthony Messenger Press, 2007), 37; see also 38-55.

7. Dogmatic Constitution on the Church, *Vatican Council II*, §22-23.

8. O'Malley, *What Happened*, 180-185, 302-305.

9. Decree on Ecumenism, *Vatican Council II*, §3.

10. Declaration on the Relationship of the Church to Non-Christian Religions, *Vatican Council II*, §2.

11. See, for example, Bokenkotter, *Concise History*, 208-213, 248-260.

12. Declaration on Religious Liberty, *Vatican Council II*, §2.

13. Hahnenberg, *Concise Guide*, offers keen insight into this fundamental issue in many of the council's debates: "If revelation itself is not primarily words *about* God, but a living encounter *with* God [as expressed in the Constitution on Divine Revelation], then we can admit that our limited human words often fail to capture this mystery. In such a view, doctrinal development is our becoming more and more conscious of all that is contained in God's offer of friendship. What is present implicitly from the beginning gradually becomes explicit in the church as we grow in our relationship with God." 153.

14. Pastoral Constitution on the Church in the Modern World, *Vatican Council II*,

§1.

15. Karl Rahner, *Concern for the Church* (New York: Crossroad, 1981), 77-102.

16. Bokenkotter, *Concise History*, 386; see also 368-386.

17. John W. O'Malley SJ, "Misdirections: Ten sure-fire ways to mix up the teaching of Vatican II," *America*, 208/3 (4 February 2013) 25-27.

18. O'Malley, "Misdirections," 25.

19. Ibid.

20. O'Malley does not give these examples in the article, but see his book, *What Happened at Vatican II*, 8-14, 254-258, 302-305.

21. Opening Message to Humanity, *The Documents of Vatican II*, 3-4.

CHAPTER 6

Catholic Morality...

Has It Changed?

Teenagers in a Catholic high school say, "It's up to the old man to decide whether it was right or wrong to kill his wife suffering from Alzheimer's disease." Some older Catholics in a parish adult-ed class express the opposite: "Just do what God tells us; just follow the Church's laws. What's all this worry about mature moral decision making?"

Very different views, aren't they? You, too, have probably wrestled with moral dilemmas: "Why be faithful to my spouse?" or "Why should I try to live a moral life in the first place? Other people don't seem to care and yet they are happy and make lots of money." Stop for a moment to reflect on just how you come to moral decisions. Along the way, maybe you also have wondered why the pope and bishops seem to be getting involved in politics and economics.

All this leads us to ask: What has happened to Catholic morality? In the years since Vatican II, there have been so many changes. Some people call it renewal; others claim the Church has gotten soft or confused. Still others emphasize the profound impact that a consumer society can have on our personal lives.

This chapter will sort through the confusion—highlighting changes from the older morality to the new, and considering the influence our culture has on our moral-decision making.

A Look Back

Christianity, of course, has always provided guidance for people's actions. Through the centuries, the Church has developed not only laws but also ways to help people make moral decisions. Those who grew up in the pre-Vatican II Church (or in its spirit) experienced a particular style of morality. For those of you not familiar with this type of morality, here is a brief summary.

Morality, at least as it was experienced by ordinary people, was usually closely connected with Confession. We reviewed the Ten Commandments and Church laws to see which ones we broke. That was sin. Of course, we knew that sin offended God, but breaking the law was more often the real focus. The laws provided crystal-clear guidance: when faced with a moral question, just find the right law and follow it. And, although it probably was never said this explicitly, many of us believed that if we followed the law, we would merit or earn our way into heaven.

Although Catholic social teaching already had quite a history, the most important issue in the popular mind seemed to be sexuality. Conscience was always discussed and respected, but the impression was given that the properly formed conscience would always follow Church teaching and laws exactly.

The clergy's training in morality also focused on Confession. Priests were taught how to help people distinguish between mortal and venial sins. The theory grounding this education was a philosophical understanding of human beings that is called the natural law. God's law, this theory held, is written in human nature. By understanding human nature properly, we could spell out the laws needed to direct our actions.

This pre-Vatican II style of morality possessed a power and clarity that directed people's lives. Law and obedience were key characteristics even though these could, and did, slip into rigidity and authoritarianism. People had a sense of the why, what, and how of Catholic morality. *Why*: to serve God and to avoid punishment (fear of hell!). *What*: the content of the laws spelled out by Church leaders about many areas of life, especially sexuality. *How*: obedience and duty to law and authority.

Let's return to our opening scenes of the teenagers and the older Catholics. The pre-Vatican II style of morality would be utterly foreign to today's teenagers in the Catholic high school. It would feel like an unfair limiting of their freedom. The teenagers' understanding and reactions, by the way, are almost certainly rooted not in the renewal of Catholic morality but in the powerful messages of our materialistic society.

On the other hand, some older persons in the parish would feel completely comfortable with this pre-Vatican II morality. It is clear, simple, secure. Well, almost. Society has had its impact on them as well. On some topics, they do not follow the pope's and bishops' guidance, mostly on issues related to politics and economics. They may support the death penalty, for example, and are suspicious of the U.S. bishops' positions expressed in their pastoral letter *Economic Justice for All*.

Vatican II's Renewal

The negative elements embedded in the pre-Vatican II style of morality — its distance from Scripture, its static view of the world, its rigidity and emphasis on obedience — gradually led people to recognize the need for renewal. First, scholars in moral theology, Scripture, and other areas of theology began planting seeds of change by their study and writings.

Then, the bishops of Vatican II made this renewal of Catholic morality an essential part of the overall renewal and reform of the Church. The council stressed: "Special attention needs to be given to the development of moral theology" (ON PRIESTLY FORMATION, §16). In its own documents, especially in *The Church in the Modern World*, Vatican II gave direction for this development: the use of Scripture, the acceptance of a worldview open to change, the role of the laity, deep respect for conscience, concern for political and economic issues.

Most important, the renewal turned from philosophy to Scripture for the foundation and center of morality. The life and teachings of Jesus, the meaning of being created in God's image and called into covenant, the rich imagination and challenge of the prophets, the cost of discipleship, the hope and vision of being an Easter people — all this provided the basis for understanding the why and what of Catholic morality. God's revelation guides us in understanding who we are and how we are to act.

The reform of moral theology also turned from the earlier view of the natural law — which emphasizes the unchangeable, the abstract, the universal — to a more modern view that understands life as historical and developing, concrete and particular. Following the lead of Saint Pope John XXIII and the Council, moral theologians read carefully "the signs of the times" and paid attention to the joys and hopes, the grief and anguish of people around the world.

Part of the renewal considered how we go about making moral decisions. Most of our choices contain positive and negative aspects. For example, saving a life may mean amputating a leg full of gangrene. Delicate discernment is central to moral-decision making. We seek to discover the right action, the one that best expresses who we are and how we are to act in light of God's revelation.

Returning again to our opening scene in the high school: the case discussed involved an elderly man who killed his ailing wife. The realism of Catholic morality demands that we discover and name what is actually happening — in this case, the taking of life. Neither a sincere intention nor just calling this action "an act of mercy" can make it so. Of course, intentions and circumstances and consequences must also be included in the evaluation, but we must begin with accurately describing the action.

Please note: Catholic tradition has justified the taking of life in some situations (for example, self-defense) but, in our case, holds that sickness and pain are not sufficient reasons to take life. "Mercy killing" (euthanasia) is *not* justified.

Why, What, How

Renewal and debate have given new insight into the why, what, and how of Catholic morality.

Why: To live in faithful, loving relationship with God, as expressed by Jesus' own example and in other great stories of the Bible, is the heart of morality. To live the moral life is to respond in love to God's call and graciousness in our lives. Sin is the breaking of that relationship. In his encyclical *The Splendor of Truth*, Saint Pope John Paul II powerfully described how following Christ is the foundation of Christian morality.

What: Scripture also helps us to appreciate the specific content of the moral life. Jesus' teachings — for example, the Good Samaritan story (LUKE 10:30-37) and the Last Judgment scene (MATT 25:31-46) — remind us of our responsibilities for other people. His Sermon on the Mount (MATT 5:1-7:29) gives us a challenging ideal to live by, even including love of our enemies. The Ten Commandments, the wisdom of the prophets, and other parts of the Hebrew Scriptures provide important guidance. Insights from Church authority, philosophy, the sciences, and human experience, of course, are also necessary.

How: Mature moral-decision making demands careful reflection, honesty, and courage. Searching for the truth in a particular situation, listening to the wisdom of authority, and praying for insight mean hard work: a willingness to discern what action best promotes human flourishing and the courage to decide.

Key Aspects of Catholic Morality

Relationship with God is the very center of morality. Jesus' own love of God and faithfulness to his call offer us the perfect model and inspiration. Our relationship with God needs to be nourished not only by personal prayer but also by participating in a Church community and its sacramental life and with a committed concern for others, especially the poor.

Morality is based on reality — God, human beings, and the rest of creation, all in relationship together. Every moral dilemma presents a small but real slice of this reality, that is, in every situation there exists a kind of objectivity — a givenness — something more than just an individual's feelings or intentions. The Catholic tradition challenges the individualism and relativism of our culture and urges us to search for the truth about moral decisions. With humility, we recognize our need to consult many and varied wisdom sources as we form our consciences.

A third key aspect is our social solidarity. We are God's daughters and sons. Every person is created in God's image, and so we respect the human dignity of all and care for all. Such a conviction often leads to a countercultural stance, with the consistent ethic of life guiding our political, social, and economic decisions. As faithful disciples and involved citizens, we must speak and act concerning welfare and immigration, sexism and racism, abortion and health care, euthanasia and the death penalty, genocide and trade agreements, and many other urgent issues.

The *Catechism*

The publication of the *Catechism of the Catholic Church* created quite a stir in the Church. The book quickly became a bestseller. Many people immediately turned to the section on morality, perhaps looking for the secure answers of the pre-Vatican II morality, perhaps hoping for expressions of the recent renewal. They found both.

The *Catechism*, as a summary of Church teachings, in fact, embodies both positive and negative aspects of Catholic moral theology. The *Catechism* follows the renewal of Vatican II by placing its whole discussion of the moral life under the title of "Life in Christ" and by rooting its view of humanity in Scripture. However, it follows the pattern of the earlier *Roman Catechism* (based on the Council of Trent, 1545–1563) by listing specific actions under the structure of the Ten Commandments rather than, for example, the Sermon on the Mount. The new *Catechism* seems to ignore its own insight that "The Beatitudes are at the heart of Jesus' preaching" (§1716) and so did not follow through on the mystery of Christ as the center of this long section of the text (§§2052–57). Similar inconsistencies are found throughout the section, especially in those areas in which the older natural law approach is favored over Vatican II's emphasis on the whole person understood in historical context. Nevertheless, the *Catechism* provides a summary of the official teaching on many of today's tough issues: genetic engineering, death penalty, violence of all kinds, sexuality, world economy, HIV/AIDS, euthanasia, and others.

Society's Influence

What has happened to Catholic morality? We have seen how Vatican II led to a profound renewal. Still, one other major influence on Catholic morality deserves attention. To appreciate what has happened to Catholic morality we must understand not only the internal dynamics of renewal and debate but also the external pressure of life in a particular culture. Here we will focus on our American life, with its technological advances and with its deeply rooted materialism and individualism.

Jesus did not have to worry about test-tube babies, genetic engineering, or respirators and other life-prolonging equipment. We do. Scientific and technological advances have clearly improved life but also raised profound questions and challenges. Moral theology has had to respond to these amazing changes and to search for the right thing to do in such new circumstances. Clearly one significant insight from all this is the absolute necessity of accurate knowledge — and so the need to consult experts of all types when dealing with such complicated issues.

Of much greater importance for our reflections on Catholic morality, however, is the influence of the materialism and individualism of our culture. The significance of this point cannot be overstated. Even as we try to live according to the gospel, we are constantly bombarded by TV, movies, music, and advertising — many of which communicate a very different set of values. Think of your favorite radio or TV programs and ask what messages about the moral life are really being communicated in them.

We may not be aware of how profoundly our morality is shaped by our culture. Most of us spend many more hours each week watching TV than going to church or reading and studying religious books. Our life in a consumer society is judged by the clothes we wear, the cars we drive, the gadgets we possess. The emphasis on the individual and individual rights pervades our contemporary society and naturally influences us. It shapes our morality, almost unconsciously. The messages sound like this: "No one can tell me what's right or wrong.... Each person must decide for himself or herself.... If it feels good, do it!"

The teenagers in our opening scene used these very words, even though they were in their eleventh year of Catholic education. Instead of carefully considering the moral implications of the action itself, this type of thinking, which is called *relativism*, holds that the individual's sincere intention is enough to make the action morally right. Pope John Paul II presented a thorough critique of relativism in his encyclical *The Splendor of Truth*.

What has happened to Catholic morality? In our culture, it has often been overshadowed or even distorted by the dominant morality of the American way of life. We may not even be aware of how our social, economic, and political systems contradict the gospel. We value things over persons, too easily turn to violence in place of peacemaking, stress retaliation rather than compassion.

Challenge and Choice

Let's return to our opening scenes and see what the why, what, and how of a renewed Catholic morality would mean for the teenagers and the older Catholics. We realize that the teenagers are at an age of seeking independence and identity. Still, their responses reveal a value system formed by modern media, not the gospel. Perhaps they are open enough to hear the challenge of recognizing that religion does have something to contribute to decisions about life and death, of realizing that good intentions alone do not determine morality. All this will take time and experience. During this time, if they are lucky, friends, family, teachers will plant seeds of the gospel vision. They might not turn to a renewed Catholic morality until they are jarred by some tragic life experience or until they have children of their own.

Some older Catholics, on the other hand, also need to be open. They have already experienced much change in their practice of the Catholic religion. But, yes, still more is asked. The safe pre-Vatican II morality is not sufficient for an adult in our world. They all must consider the moral ambiguities present in our everyday world, the demands of a justice inspired by faith.

Catholic morality has experienced a profound and rich renewal, inviting all of us into deeper love, trust, discernment, and dedicated action in our day-to-day lives. Catholic morality is also threatened by rigidity and the fear of change and especially by the materialism and relativism of our culture. The challenge of the choice of value systems faces each of us. In his encyclical *The Gospel of Life*, Pope John Paul II dramatically described this choice as a choice between a "culture of life" and a "culture of death." *Choose life!*

CHAPTER 7

A Consistent Ethic of Life

Everyone knows there is darkness in our lives, in our world. Violence of all kinds threatens life: in our homes, in our cities, in nations near and far.

> Violence has many faces: oppression of the poor, depriva-
> tion of basic human rights, economic exploitation, sexual
> exploitation and pornography, neglect or abuse of the
> aged and the helpless, and innumerable other acts of in-
> humanity. Abortion in particular blunts a sense of the sa-
> credness of human life.[1]

We see this passage from the U.S. bishops' 1983 pastoral letter on peace exemplified almost every day in the headlines. Many of us have directly encountered some form of violence in our own lives. Many more of us suffer with families and friends who have. How can we respond to this violence and death? How can we oppose evil without creating new evils and becoming evil ourselves?

A moral vision that holds together these many different issues and offers not only direction for action but also energy and hope is the consistent ethic of life. The late Cardinal Joseph Bernardin (1928-1996) articulated this perspective in the early 1980s, and it became a centerpiece of the U.S. Catholic bishops' moral teaching. Though it has not been emphasized in recent statements by the U.S. bishops, we would do well to retrieve the consistent ethic of life, both its content and spirit. Saint Pope John Paul II affirmed similar themes in his 1995 encyclical *The Gospel of Life*.[2] In this chapter, we will explore the richness of this teaching.

A Moral Framework

What is the consistent ethic of life? It is a comprehensive ethical system that links together many different issues by focusing attention on the basic value of life. In his attempts to defend life, Cardinal Bernardin first joined the topics of abortion and nuclear war. He quickly expanded his understanding of a consistent ethic of life to include many issues from all of life. In the first of a series of talks, Cardinal Bernardin stated: "The spectrum of life cuts across the issues of genetics, abortion, capital punishment, modern warfare, and the care of the terminally ill".[3]

Cardinal Bernardin also acknowledged that issues are distinct and different. Capital punishment, for example, is not the same as abortion. Nevertheless, the issues are linked. The valuing and defense of life are at the center of both issues. Cardinal Bernardin told an audience in Portland, Oregon: "When human life is considered 'cheap' or easily expendable in one area, eventually nothing is held as sacred and all lives are in jeopardy."

Along with his consistent linking of distinct life issues, Cardinal Bernardin acknowledged that no individual or group can pursue all issues. Still, while concentrating on one issue, he insisted in another address, the individual or group must not be seen "as insensitive to or even opposed to other moral claims on the overall spectrum of life." The consistent ethic of life rules out contradictory moral positions about the unique value of human life — and it would be contradictory, for example, to be *against* abortion but *for* capital punishment or to work against poverty but support euthanasia.

This linkage of all life issues is, of course, the very heart of the consistent ethic of life. This linking challenges us to pull together things that we might have kept apart in the past. Often our convictions seem to cluster around "conservative" or "liberal" viewpoints — as in the above examples. But the consistent ethic of life cuts across such divisions, calling us to respect the life in the womb, the life of a criminal, the life on welfare, the life of the dying.

Sources of Life

Where does the consistent ethic of life come from? It comes largely from the insights of Cardinal Bernardin, the teachings of the U.S. Catholic bishops, and Pope John Paul II's encyclical *The Gospel of Life*. The ultimate source, however, is the Bible, especially the life and teaching of Jesus.

Cardinal Bernardin spent much time and energy on two issues: abortion and nuclear war. He found committed people concerned about one issue but not the other. As he worked to bring together those seeking an end to abortion and those trying to prevent nuclear war, Cardinal Bernardin began to emphasize the common link among the life issues. This emphasis was continued in the teachings of the U.S. bishops.

Pope John Paul II's encyclical *The Gospel of Life* is a bold and prophetic defense of life. Although it does not use the phrase "the consistent ethic of life," *The Gospel of Life* strongly affirms this concept. John Paul describes what is going on in our world today: a monumental abuse of life through drugs, war and arms, abortion, euthanasia, destruction of the environment, unjust distribution of resources. This abuse is often caused and supported by the economic, social and political structures of the nations. So the pope speaks of a "structure of sin" and a "culture of death" and a "conspiracy against life" (§12).

The pope also proclaims the Christian understanding of the value of life. Created in God's image, redeemed by Jesus, called to everlasting life, every human being is sacred and social; every human being is a sign of God's love. In much more detail than Cardinal Bernardin's addresses, the pope provides the foundation for building a culture of life by weaving together a wealth of biblical texts that clearly proclaim human dignity.

The consistent ethic of life is ultimately rooted in Jesus, in whom the meaning and value of life are definitively proclaimed and fully given. In John Paul II's words, "The gospel of life is not simply a reflection, however new and profound, on human life. Nor is it merely a commandment aimed at raising awareness and bringing about significant changes in society. Still less is it an illusory promise of a better future. The gospel of life is something concrete and personal, for it consists in the proclamation of *the very person of Jesus*" (§29).

Who is this Jesus? He is Jesus who was sensitive to the vulnerable at all stages and from every walk of life. In being so, he often was at odds with society's standards, associating with religious and social outcasts. This is the Jesus of the Sermon on the Mount who proclaims as blessed not the leaders of society but the mourning and the meek, the poor and the pure, the persecuted and the peacemaker (MATT 5:1-12).

This is the Jesus who praises not power but reconciliation in the story about the forgiving father of the prodigal son (LUKE 15:11-32). This is the Jesus of faithful ministry, of suffering and death, of new life (MARK 14:3-16:8). This is the Jesus who says, "I came so that they might have life and have it more abundantly" (JOHN 10:10). Who Jesus is and what Jesus means by abundant life, then, are surely different from what the consumerism and individualism of our culture tell us about life.

Abundant Life

The consistent ethic of life challenges us every day. (1) It encourages us to hold together a great variety of issues with a consistent focus on the value of life. (2) It challenges us to reflect on our basic values and convictions that give direction to our lives. (3) It leads us to express our commitment to life in civil debate and public policy.

From womb to tomb. A consistent ethic includes all life issues from the very beginning of life to its end. An excellent example of how the life ethic holds together many distinct issues can be found in the U.S. bishops' 1996 statement, *Political Responsibility*, that provided direction concerning many issues, including abortion, racism, the economy, AIDS, housing, the global trade in arms, welfare reform, immigration, and refugees.

Several examples can give the spirit of *Political Responsibility* and help us examine our consciences. The bishops oppose the use of the death penalty, judging that the practice further undermines respect for life in our society and stating that it has been discriminatory against the poor and racial minorities. The bishops express special concern for the problem of racism, calling it a "radical evil" that divides the human family. Dealing with poverty, the bishops claim, is a moral imperative of the highest priority for poverty threatens life. In the domestic scene, there is a need for more jobs with adequate pay and decent working conditions; at the international level, the areas of trade, aid, and investment must be reevaluated in terms of their impact on the poor.

Capital punishment, racism, poverty: certainly these are very different issues, with different causes and different solutions (many that may be very complex). Still, underneath all these differences is life and, for us, the challenge of respecting the lives of people who may be very different from us. What actions concerning these issues would a consistent ethic of life suggest?

Here are a few possibilities. For capital punishment, spend time learning why many churches are opposed to the death penalty; then write to your governor and other officials expressing your opposition. For racism, start or join a parish group that is working to bring together people of different races, perhaps by a formal, ongoing interchange between two parishes ("twinning"). For poverty, read the bishops' pastoral letter *Economic Justice for All*; volunteer in a soup kitchen or an AIDS clinic; if possible, exercise your leadership in business or politics to change oppressive policies and regulations. Surely, we cannot do everything, but we can do one thing.

A question of values. The consistent ethic of life also leads us beyond the specific issues to the depths of our convictions about the meaning of life. A careful and prayerful study of *Political Responsibility* allows us to appreciate not only the expanse of the seamless garment of the consistent ethic of life but also its profound challenge to our most important attitudes and values.

Emphasizing the consistent ethic of life and recognizing its counter-cultural directions, the bishops state: "Our moral framework does not easily fit the categories of right or left, Republican or Democrat. We are called to measure every party and movement by how its agenda touches human life and human dignity."

It is not sufficient to be pro-life on some issues; we must be pro-life on all issues — no matter what our political party, business, union, talk shows, advertising, or family may say. These powerful forces significantly shape our values and convictions, sometimes away from a consistent ethic. Yet our faith ought to be the deepest source of our values.

We should not underestimate the challenge of being pro-life; it might seem easier to appeal to common sense or accepted business practice — or even ethical relativism. In *The Gospel of Life*, Saint John Paul II urges all persons to choose life — consistently, personally, nationally, globally. This invitation is really a profound challenge: to look deeply into ourselves and to test against the gospel some of our own deeply held beliefs and practices.

John Paul writes: "In a word, we can say that the cultural change which we are calling for demands from everyone the courage to *adopt a new lifestyle,* consisting in making practical choices — at the personal, family, social and international level — on the basis of a correct scale of values: *the primacy of being over having, of the person over things.* This renewed lifestyle involves a passing *from indifference to concern for others, from rejection to acceptance of them"* (§98).

Public policy. Our Church leaders have necessarily discussed the relationship between moral vision and political policies. Indeed, the consistent ethic of life was developed to help shape public policy. Political policies and economic structures provide means to create a societal environment that promotes the flourishing of human life. During the past century, bishops and popes have addressed these very issues in their social teachings.

As Cardinal Bernardin told the audience at Fordham University, we must also be able to state our case "in nonreligious terms which others of different faith convictions might find morally persuasive." For example, we may be opposed to euthanasia and assisted suicide fundamentally because of our faith convictions about God as giver of the gift of life and about our own stewardship of life. For public policy discussion, however, we may stress other reasons, such as human dignity, the undermining of trust in the medical profession, the threat to women and the vulnerable.

Political Responsibility and *The Gospel of Life* emphasize that faithfulness to the gospel leads not only to individual acts of charity. It also leads to actions involving the institutions and structures of society, the economy, and politics. The U.S. bishops, for example, state:

> We encourage people to use their voices and votes to enrich the democratic life of our nation and to act on their values in the political arena. We hope American Catholics, as both believers and citizens, will use the resources of our faith and the opportunities of this democracy to help shape a society more respectful of the life, dignity and rights of the human person, especially the poor and vulnerable.

Clearly, religion and politics must mix in our lives! We face the challenge of consistently embodying an ethic of life in the candidates we support and in our own direct involvement in forming public policy (whether that be in the Girl Scouts, in a parish committee, in a local school board, or in the U.S. Congress).

Discipleship's Challenge

In this new millennium, world events and Church teachings direct our attention to life itself as the very center of our concern. The consistent ethic of life provides both a solid foundation and a powerful challenge to live as faithful disciples and involved citizens. It calls into question all views that contradict the message and meaning of Jesus. It challenges us to reject the culture of death. It challenges us to create a culture of life every day, at home, at work, and in society.

How? The way we vote, the jokes we tell, the language we use, the attitudes we hand on to children, the causes we support, the business practices we use, the entertainment we attend, the way we care for the sick and elderly — in all these ordinary activities, we express consistency in respecting life or we get trapped in contradictions.

If we are consistent, we must speak and act concerning abortion and euthanasia but also concerning welfare and immigration, sexism and racism, cloning and health care reform, trade agreements and sweatshops, the buying and selling of women for prostitution, genocide, and many other issues. Based on our ancient Scriptures and attentive to contemporary experiences, the consistent ethic of life provides an ethical framework for confronting the moral dilemmas of our new millennium. It helps us to promote the full flourishing of all life.

ENDNOTES

1. *The Challenge of Peace: God's Promise and Our Response, A Pastoral Letter on War and Peace*, National Conference of Catholic Bishops, http://www.usccb.org/upload/challenge-peace-gods-promise-our-response-1983.pdf, 3 May 1983.

2. John Paul II, *The Gospel of Life (Humanae Vitaae)*, encyclical, http://w2.vatican.va/content/john-paul-ii/en/encyclicals/documents/hf_jp-ii_enc_25031995_evangelium-vitae.html, 25 March 1995.

3. Joseph Cardinal Bernardin, lecture, Fordham University, New York, 6 December 1983.

CHAPTER 8

125 Years of Catholic Social Teaching
Guidance for a Troubled World

As we celebrated the 125th anniversary of the landmark encyclical, *The Condition of Labor* (*Rerum Novarum*), both old and new social, political, and economic events continued to rock our world: genocide, terrorism, AIDS, preemptive war, refugees, globalization, worldwide economic crises.

In the midst of these threats to hope and to life itself, we have discovered the continuing wisdom and urgency of Catholic social teaching. Its emphasis and guidance remain relevant, real, and challenging.

The collection of documents called the social teachings began in 1891 with Pope Leo XIII's *The Condition of Labor*. For more than 125 years, the statements of the popes, Vatican II, and conferences of bishops have addressed critical national and international issues such as human rights, labor problems, economic depression and development, political participation, war and peace.

In recent years, Pope Benedict XVI in his first encyclical, *God Is Love* (*Deus Caritas Est*), affirmed the wisdom of the social teachings while discussing the relationship between justice and charity. He states that "the promotion of justice through efforts to bring about openness of mind and will to the demands of the common good is something which concerns the church deeply" (§28A).

In a later encyclical, *Charity in Truth* (*Caritas in Veritate*), Pope Benedict addresses issues of social ethics, especially the financial crisis and related topics. He states his basic conviction this way: "The greatest service to development, then, is a Christian humanism that enkindles charity and takes its lead from truth, accepting both as a lasting gift from God" (§78). The pope offers many applications, such as, "projects for integral human development cannot ignore coming generations, but need to be marked by solidarity and *inter-generational justice*, while taking into account a variety of contexts: ecological, juridical, economic, political and cultural" (§48).

Most recently Pope Francis challenged the world about the environmental crisis in his *Laudato Si: On Care for Our Common Home*. This encyclical calls for an ecological conversion, indeed, for a profound change in lifestyle.

To help us all follow Pope Paul VI's words that these social questions "must in the years to come take first place among the preoccupations of Christians" (A CALL TO ACTION, §7), this chapter will explore five major themes of the Church's social teaching and offer some action steps for today.

1. Affirming Human Dignity

At the heart of Catholic social teaching is an emphasis on the value of the human being. We are created in God's image, and our value is rooted fundamentally in who we are and not in what we do.

Situations that undermine or limit human dignity cry out for change; those that truly promote such dignity need to be fostered. The theme of human dignity is discussed in detail in two documents: (1) Saint Pope John XXIII's *Peace on Earth* presents the more philosophical view and (2) Vatican II's *The Church in the Modern World* sets forth the more scriptural view.

Pope John XXIII develops at length his conviction that human nature provides the key both for individual rights and duties and for the international cooperation necessary for peace. *The Church in the Modern World* incorporates much of Pope John's thought but emphasizes how the Bible shows the meaning of human dignity: in Jesus Christ, sin is overcome and each person's full dignity and destiny are revealed.

Action Steps

What does this emphasis on human dignity mean for us? At least three things:

1. *See human dignity as a starting point for moral decision making.* Our growing appreciation of what truly enriches human dignity — and what truly injures it — provides a solid basis for our morality.

2. *Believe in your own worth.* The social teachings remind us that we, too, are precious and unique.

3. *Treat others with great respect.* Too easily, we get trapped in thinking of others according to some stereotype, especially those who are different from us. We need to skip the racist joke and the sexist comment.

2. Valuing Work

Labor — or better, the *laborer* — has been a central theme of the social teachings. In 1891, Pope Leo XIII wrote *The Condition of Labor* in response to the massive problems caused by the Industrial Revolution: exploitation of the worker, terrible working conditions, unjust wages. In order to defend people from such abuse, Leo stresses the basic right of human beings to work, to receive a just wage, to form unions, to possess private property.

Concern for the worker is expressed throughout the social teachings and is developed in detail in a contemporary way in Saint Pope John Paul II's *On Human Work*. In this very reflective statement, the pope again affirms the rights of workers and unions.

Consistent with other social teachings, *On Human Work* criticizes Marxism with its emphasis on state ownership and its rejection of private property; it also criticizes capitalism for its neglect of the common good and for its focus on productivity and profit rather than people.

Action Steps

The social teachings prompt the following suggestions:

1. *Take a fresh look at your work.* Most of us work, but do we really find our work creative and fulfilling, or does it more often become numbing drudgery?

2. *Be attentive to questions of justice at your workplace.* In the U.S., working conditions and the power of unions have changed drastically in the many years since *The Condition of Labor*. Our view of the relationship between workers and owners probably depends much more on our profession and economic bracket than on the social teachings.

3. *Recognize both values and limits in capitalism.* Pope John Paul II stresses both in his encyclical *Centesimus Annus* commemorating the 100th anniversary of *The Condition of Labor*. While some commentators try to interpret his words as a complete affirmation of capitalism, John Paul actually offers a powerful critique of capitalism, with its domination of things over people and the worsening problems of marginalization, consumerism, and exploitation.

3. Developing the Common Good

Closely related to concern for workers and international economics is the third major theme: the common good. Recognizing the increasing interdependence among all the peoples on earth, Pope John XXIII explains in *Peace on Earth* that the universal common good "embraces the sum total of those conditions of social living whereby people are enabled to achieve their own integral perfection more fully and more easily" (§58).

Such basic necessities as food, clothing, and shelter are, of course, included, but also the right to education, the right to take an active part in public affairs, the right to worship God freely.

Pope John argues that in today's world the common good of one nation cannot be separated from the common good of the whole human family. Countries must seek the good of all and not just their own self-interest.

Later popes continue to develop this theme of international development and liberation. Pope John Paul II's *On Social Concern* commemorates the twentieth anniversary of Paul VI's *The Development of Peoples*. Pope

John Paul judges that the reality of the developing nations has become worse in the intervening twenty years and so calls for genuine collaboration among peoples as a necessary part of our response.

Although earlier popes had addressed concerns about the environment, Pope Francis is the first to devote an entire encyclical to the topic. Issues include pollution, water, climate change, and global inequality. A perfect example of the common good: the very existence of "our common home."

Action Steps

Especially at this point, we may be tempted to ask, "What can I do? I'm only one individual." Worldwide political, economic, and environmental issues are immense and overwhelming. The social teachings, however, stand as a challenge to us, reminding us that it is our world and, in some sense, our responsibility.

1. *Develop a global outlook.* In our families, for example, we can discuss and pray over issues like famines or global warming or the pain of whole nations torn by strife. We could also express our global concerns in the way we vote and by writing those who represent us in Congress.

2. *Find ways to promote the common good.* For instance, we North Americans might raise our awareness of how a consumer-oriented lifestyle affects other nations: How does the gobbling up of shrinking supplies of oil and lumber by some nations, for example, deplete the resources and harm the environment of others? This might lead us to personal efforts to conserve the earth's resources: by recycling, perhaps, or simplifying our lifestyles.

4. Creating Justice

Justice — right relationships along with the structural recognition of human dignity and rights and responsibilities — is a major theme throughout the social teachings.

In 1971, a worldwide synod of bishops met to follow Vatican II's direction to "read the signs of the times." The synod's statement, *Justice in the World*, finds massive divisions in the world between rich and poor, which result in millions of people living marginal lives, being illiterate, ill-fed, and poorly housed. The bishops state that the gospel demands justice for these people as an essential expression of Christian love. Our relationship with God is closely related to our relationship with other persons.

In a celebrated passage of this statement, the bishops declare: "Action on behalf of justice and participation in the transformation of the world fully appear to us as a constitutive dimension of the preaching of the gospel" (§6).

In *A Call to Action*, Pope Paul VI addresses other justice concerns including urbanization, discrimination, the role of women, the environment. Concerning women, for example, Paul asserts that "developments in legislation should...be directed to...recognizing her independence as a person, and her equal rights to participate in cultural, economic, social and political life" (§13).

He addresses the environment too: "Humanity is suddenly becoming aware that by an ill-considered exploitation of nature humans risk destroying it and becoming in turn the victim of this degradation" (§21).

Action Steps

Here are some ways that we can help to create a more just society:

1. *Get involved in political issues.* When we see how some government and business leaders make decisions that oppress people and deny human dignity (think of corporate scandals in the U.S., and sweatshops everywhere) we cannot, as Christians, simply remain silent about these profoundly human, ethical, religious issues. We see the importance of voting responsibly and speaking out on such matters. The people whom we elect are the ones determining policy on a wide range of crucial justice issues, whether it is a matter of trade agreements, funds to fight AIDS and malaria, or the debts of poor countries.

2. *Start now in your home and community.* There are plenty of justice questions to tackle in our own backyards. Do we abandon the elderly in nursing homes? Do we scornfully look down on persons suffering mental illness? Are we prejudiced against persons of a different sexual orientation or race or religion? How are our attitudes embodied in our votes on bond issues and school policies or in decisions about volunteering? We don't have to look far to find people and places in need of justice.

5. Building Peace

In a century marked by world wars, the use of atomic bombs and the build-up of arms, the social teachings frequently turned to the topic of war and peace. As we have already seen, Pope John XXIII's *Peace on Earth* emphasizes human dignity, rights, and duties as the only possible foundation for true peace.

Vatican II's *Church in the Modern World* links the preparation for war with the problems of development: "The arms race is one of the greatest curses on the human race and the harm it inflicts upon the poor is more than can be endured" (§81).

Pope John Paul II states: "Peace is not just the absence of war. It involves mutual respect and confidence between peoples and nations. It involves collaboration and binding agreements. Like a cathedral, peace must be constructed patiently and with unshakable faith" (Homily at Coventry Cathedral, quoted in the U.S. bishops' pastoral letter *The Challenge of Peace*, §200).

As the twenty-first century began with terrorism and preemptive war, Pope John Paul more and more limited the application of just-war theory and emphasized the necessity of creating peace. In his address to the Diplomatic Corps in 2003, he states: "War is not always inevitable. It is always a defeat for humanity." Solutions in the Middle East "will never be imposed by recourse to terrorism or armed conflict, as if military victories could be the solution."

Action Steps

How can we help?

1. *Be a peacemaker in your community.* The bishops conclude their long pastoral letter by urging Christians to accept the cost of discipleship, to be faithful to gospel values. Concretely, this may mean helping to resolve conflicts at work or home or teaching children a message of peace when we see violence on TV.

2. *See the link between war and other human violations. The Challenge of Peace* shows connections between preparation for war and all the other issues treated in this article: "When we accept violence, war itself can be taken for granted. Violence has many faces: oppression of the poor, deprivation of basic human rights, economic exploitation, sexual exploitation and pornography, neglect or abuse of the aged and the helpless, and innumerable other acts of inhumanity. Abortion in particular blunts a sense of the sacredness of human life" (§285).

Challenge and Hope

Our rich heritage of Catholic social teachings challenges us to use our gifts and imagination in upholding the dignity of people and tackling the social problems of our day as active citizens.

The Church, moreover, proclaims its profound trust that a loving God walks with us. As the U.S. bishops' Economic Justice for All puts it: "We cannot be frightened by the magnitude and complexity of these problems. We must not be discouraged.... [A]s believers in the redemptive love of God and as those who have experienced God's forgiving mercy, we know that God's providence is not and will not be lacking to us" (§364).

APPENDIX: SOME KEY SOCIAL TEACHINGS

1891 Leo XIII, **The Condition of Labor** (*Rerum Novarum*): addresses the pressing problems of industrialization and the oppression of workers.

1931 Pius XI, **The Reconstruction of the Social Order** (*Quadragesimo Anno*): responds to the impact of the economic depression: affirms just wages and unions; condemns unequal distribution of wealth; opposes both unrestricted capitalism and Marxism.

1961 John XXIII, **Christianity and Social Progress** (*Mater et Magistra*): turns to global interdependence and the vast differences between rich and poor nations.

1963 John XXIII, **Peace on Earth** (*Pacem in Terris*): presents a detailed analysis of human dignity and rights; affirms democracy and the rights of press, speech, and religion.

1965 Vatican II, **Pastoral Constitution on the Church in the Modern World** (*Gaudium et Spes*): emphasizes the scriptural views of the human person; addresses critical issues of marriage, culture, economics, politics, war and peace.

1967 Paul VI, **The Development of Peoples** (*Populorum Progressio*): explores the deeper meaning of development—cultural, social, religious needs, along with economic ones; urges fair trade relations and other forms of international cooperation.

1971 Paul VI, **A Call to Action** (*Octogesima Adveniens*): focuses on political power and justice.

1971 Synod of Bishops, **Justice in the World**: stresses the preferential option for the poor and the reform of society so that all persons are able to participate actively in the economic, political, and cultural life of their society.

1981 John Paul II, **On Human Work** (*Laborem Exercens*): emphasizes the primacy of people over things; develops a spirituality of work.

1987 John Paul II, **On Social Concern** (*Sollicitudo Rei Socialis*): discusses the massive economic gap between North and South (in terms of global hemispheres); urges redirection of resources from producing arms to alleviating misery of impoverished peoples.

1991 John Paul II, **On the Hundredth Anniversary of Rerum Novarum** (*Centesimus Annus*): indicates how key themes of Leo XIII's encyclical remain valid for today's world; affirms and critiques capitalism, as shown in John Sniegocki's *Horizons* article, "The Social Ethics of Pope John Paul II."

1995 John Paul II, **The Gospel of Life** (*Evangelium Vitae*): defends life from womb to tomb, discussing abortion, euthanasia, self-defense, the death penalty, and the relationship between civil and moral law.

2009 Benedict XVI, **Charity in Truth** (*Caritas in Veritate*): marks the fortieth anniversary of Paul VI's *The Development of Peoples*; addresses the global financial crisis and discusses positive and negative aspects of globalization.

2015 Francis, **Praise Be to You** (*Laudato Si*): addresses the ecological crisis facing "our common home." Issues include pollution, water, climate change, and global inequality.

CHAPTER 9

Wisdom from Sunday Readings

#1 Emmaus and Our Vision of Life

Horrors abound. Terrorism around the world, followed by violent response in an attempt to end violence. The ever-deepening cycle of retaliation among religious and ethnic groups. Many forms of racism and other prejudices. Scandals in the church.

How are we responding to these horrors? Often with shock and anger, outrage and bitterness. Just listen to politicians. Read editorials, commentaries, and letters to the editors. Tune in to news broadcasts and radio talk-shows.

While shock and outrage may be natural responses to these horrors, we who want to live as disciples of Jesus must also ask if we ought to act on these feelings. What guidance do the teachings and life of Jesus offer us for our actions?

At the heart of Jesus' ministry is his vision of the reign of God. The Gospels clearly describe its characteristics: compassion and forgiveness, joy and trust, surprising goodness and care for the poor, nonviolence and love of enemies.

Jesus' vision of life in God's reign challenges our instinctive and "common-sense" responses to the many horrors in our world. Jesus' teachings confront us with the possibility that our appeals for justice are really cries for vengeance, that patriotism may be a mask for violent self-interest. Jesus calls us to transformed and transforming actions that resist evil nonviolently and promote the flourishing of all life.

Is it possible? With God's help, of course! We must recognize, however, the deep influence of media and politics and economics that suggest other values and so shape our consciences. Every Easter season (especially the Third Sunday in Year A) offers us a grace-filled alternative: the story of Emmaus. Luke's wonderful account (chapter 24) of the transformation of the two despairing disciples is undoubtedly the story of the early Christian community, remembering Jesus, understanding and living the Scriptures in a new way, recognizing the risen Jesus' presence in the breaking of the bread.

Emmaus is also *our* story. We need to return again and again to the Eucharist, our Emmaus, to experience solidarity in living and proclaiming the countercultural values of the reign of God, to be nourished by the Bread of Life. We need vibrant parishes and liturgies to enlighten, challenge, sustain us. In light of this need, we see that scandals in the church are especially damaging. Great harm is done both to the victims and to the whole church.

Still, it is the Eucharist that offers us a privileged place for meeting God, finding reconciliation, and nurturing hope. How urgently we need to hear and live the words of an Eucharistic Prayer for Reconciliation: "In the midst of conflict and division, we know it is you, ever-living God, who turn our minds to thoughts of peace. Your Spirit changes our hearts: enemies begin to speak to one another, those who were estranged join hands in friendship, and nations seek the way of peace together. Your Spirit is at work when understanding puts an end to strife, when hatred is quenched by mercy, and vengeance gives way to forgiveness."

Along with this deep formation of our life and values, we also need information, including other sources than mainstream media. Many statements from our bishops can help guide us. Also recommended are *America* and *The Tablet* and materials from Pax Christi and Bread for the World.

In what vision of life are your deepest values and commitments really rooted?

#2 No Forbidden Questions

Some scripture passages console and comfort us, for example numerous passages from Second Isaiah (Cн 40-55) or from Jesus' last discourse (John 14-17). Other passages are complex and even troublesome. Such are the readings for the Twenty-seventh Sunday in Ordinary Time in year B.[1] An important theme of these readings is our significant relationships: with other humans, especially one's spouse; with creation; and with God. But just what is the meaning of God's word in these selections?

Words of Bishop Karl Lehmann and Albert Raffelt, used to introduce Karl Rahner's *The Practice of Faith*, offer a helpful perspective for pondering this collection of scriptures. "God's response never fails to transcend our capacity to ask questions, and the spiritually alert Christian ... must continue to swing the hard, sober hammer of inquiry. There are no forbidden questions, then, nor any false pride in some inviolable, final 'possession' of understanding."[2]

Sober inquiry that is both faithful and creative can offer us fruitful interpretations of the scriptures and wisdom about the implications for these vital relationships.

The first reading is from the second — and older — creation story in Genesis. While it stresses that woman has a similar nature to man, it has been interpreted to say that woman's existence, psychologically and in the social order, is dependent on man. We recognize how profound and painful this issue is.

The respect for the dignity and rights of women has certainly increased in many places, though often only through tense struggle. Various scripture passages have been and still are used to subjugate and abuse women (for example, Eph 5:22). Much sober inquiry is needed. We must struggle to discover how appreciation for religious and cultural traditions can be combined with true respect for the dignity of women. By highlighting Jesus' relationships with women, especially in the Gospel According to Luke, contemporary scripture scholarship can help challenge those traditions when they are rooted in unexamined assumptions that result in the oppression of women.

Genesis also directs our attention to our relationship with all of creation. In this passage the man's naming each being (Gen 2:19, 20) has often been understood in terms of "dominion" (see Gen 1:26). We know how the creation stories in Genesis have been used to justify not only humanity's domination of the rest of creation but also its abuse.

Despite mounting evidence that climate change threatens the earth and all life, some still deny its reality. In response, along with the continuing scientific inquiry, we must find ways to promote popular education and to challenge political policies and economic structures that damage the environment. There must be no forbidden questions. We can join together to inspire a deepening awareness about stewardship of earth.[3] Religious groups in particular can foster a renewed understanding of Genesis (*care* for creation rather than *abuse* of it) and help people realize that climate change, as a real threat to all life, is the fundamental pro-life concern. There is no more important moral issue than the very existence of humanity.

The second reading, beginning a series of passages from the letter to the Hebrews, raises questions about God. This letter—actually a written sermon—exhorts a community in crisis to persevere in hope and faith. Its focus, rooted in interpretations of the Hebrew Scriptures, is on Christ as the unique, eternal high priest and as the model of faith. This passage presents the familiar theory of expiation, that God willed Jesus' suffering and death for the sake of all. An understandable theory in the context, but one that seems to contradict Jesus' own vision of God.

The mystery of God has always prompted serious inquiry. Scripture scholarship has helped us appreciate Jesus' intimate, loving relationship with Abba God. Jesus preaches nonviolence and a God of compassion and forgiveness. Jesus' God sends the rain on the just and the unjust (see Matt 5:43-48). Through the centuries, some theologians (for example, the Cappadocians, Duns Scotus, Teilhard de Chardin, Schillebeeckx, and Karl Rahner) have described this gracious God sharing life and love in creation and in incarnation. Still, popular piety and preaching prefer a god who sends Jesus to suffer and die (as in the text from Hebrews). Too easily such a view presents an image of a vindictive god. As parents, priests, and teachers, we can learn the tradition closer to Jesus' own experience,[4] helping us to abandon the conviction in theology and in society that violence saves.

Finally, the gospel passage presents Jesus' teaching on divorce, as modified by the evangelist. Mark adapts Jesus' conviction to the Gentile world, adding the part about a woman divorcing her husband. Jesus would not have said that, because Jewish women could not divorce Jewish men.

In our context today, we are acutely aware of the suffering in unhealthy marriages and the challenges concerning divorce. We search for ways to be faithful to Jesus' vision and to be compassionate and wise. As we learn from the painful experience of good and faithful people, we must develop appropriate pastoral responses that promote authentic human flourishing. Theological inquiry must recognize that there are no forbidden questions as it investigates with creative fidelity the implications of Vatican II's emphasis on marriage as a covenant and not just a contract.

The scriptures from an ordinary Sunday open up the depths of human life, revealing serious and challenging issues. Consider the significant relationships in your life—with your spouse, other persons, all of creation, God. Where do you need to swing the hard, sober hammer of inquiry?

#3 Freeing Forgiveness: Making a Twofold Decision

The Scriptures for the Eleventh Sunday in Ordinary Time (Year C) offer us a profound challenge concerning forgiveness.[5] The first reading from Samuel presents a list of dramatic sins of David and then concludes with a simple confession and statement of forgiveness. Luke's gospel, in contrast, simply identifies the uninvited dinner guest as a known sinner, but describes in detail her extravagant expressions of love in anointing Jesus. This scandalous act takes place during a dinner at the house of Simon the Pharisee.

Though Jesus is better known for his meals with various types of marginalized folks, here he dines with a respected member of society. Table fellowship expresses the inclusivity of God's reign: both outcasts and Pharisees. While our attention easily turns to the woman, Jesus' exchange with Simon is just as noteworthy.

Luke describes Simon as rejecting Jesus as a prophet because Jesus allows this sinner to touch him, violating social conventions and making Jesus unclean. Jesus not only responds as a prophet, reading Simon's thoughts, but more than a prophet in confirming that the woman's sins had been forgiven.

In his response to Simon, Jesus tells the story of two people in debt and a generous creditor who forgave both. Simon recognizes that the one who was forgiven more would love more. Jesus contrasts the woman's generous actions with Simon's lack of hospitality. But then Simon disappears from Luke's account. As with the older brother and his response to his forgiving father in Luke's story of the prodigal son, we do not know how Simon responded to Jesus' challenge. Did Simon recognize his self-righteousness and seek forgiveness? Did he too experience freedom to love extravagantly? Perhaps Luke was hoping that some members of his community would see themselves in Simon and so ponder their own response.

Jesus turns his attention to the woman, celebrating her change of heart: "her many sins have been forgiven; hence she has shown great love" (7:47). Forgiveness set her free to love.[6]

For a great variety of reasons, like David and Simon and the unnamed woman, we all have an urgent need in our lives both for forgiveness and for the capacity to forgive. The need is overwhelming, from deep personal wounds to alienation in families and marriages to hatred and suspicion between ethnic groups to abuse of children in our church to a world of massive violence.

In this context, Christians still pray frequently: Forgive us our trespasses as we forgive those who trespass against us. Do we really pay attention to our own prayer? We may be blind to our sinfulness or simply too complacent to acknowledge honestly our trespasses/debts and our need for forgiveness. Jesus' challenging invitation to Simon is then particularly fitting for us too. Despite our prayer, we may also find it hard to forgive others or ourselves. In another place in his gospel, Luke even describes Jesus broadening the scope of forgiveness, proclaiming that it must be limitless (17:4; SEE ALSO MATT 18:21-22). Jesus' vision is rooted in his conviction that God is a compassionate and forgiving God who cares for all people, a conviction that we may not yet fully share or trust.

So what exactly is forgiveness? Some years ago, an insightful article appeared in the weekly U.S. magazine *America* attempting to answer this question.[7] Before the sexual abuse crisis in the church in the United States intensified in 2002, there was a case of a lay director of religious education accused of molesting youth from his parish in Massachusetts. The local district attorney speculated that as many as 250 youth may have been molested.

In this context of horror, Stephen Pope described forgiveness as a moral act based on a religious vision. "To 'forgive' in the Christian sense, then, means to make a twofold decision. Negatively, it means to renounce hatred and the desire to destroy; positively, it means to will what is morally good to one who has been harmful.... Christian forgiveness intends healing and transformation."[8] Because of the deep pain, forgiveness is not easy. It takes time and cannot be rushed. It does not ignore the evil, nor does it deny the natural feelings of anger. Christian forgiveness chooses to move past these feelings. It is "the deliberate *decision*, or, really, the commitment to decide over and over again, to extend good will to one who has done evil."[9] Christian forgiveness imitates the unlimited range of God's forgiveness.

Two years later, following the 9/11 attacks, Saint Pope John Paul II expressed similar thoughts in his message for World Peace Day (January 1, 2002). His title, "No Peace Without Justice, No Justice Without Forgiveness," accurately indicates the heart of the pope's challenging message. He calls forgiveness a personal choice, "a decision of the heart to go against the natural instinct to pay back evil with evil.... The ability to forgive lies at the very basis of the idea of a future society marked by justice and solidarity."[10]

As if anticipating people's rejection of the possibility of forgiveness, John Paul states:

> Forgiveness is not a proposal that can be immediately understood or easily accepted; in many ways it is a paradoxical message. Forgiveness in fact always involves an apparent short-term loss for a real long-term gain. Violence is the exact opposite; opting as it does for an apparent short-term gain, it involves a real and permanent loss. Forgiveness may seem like weakness, but it demands great spiritual strength and moral courage, both in granting it and in accepting it.[11]

Giving and receiving forgiveness frees us to love, even to love extravagantly as did the woman in Luke's gospel. Perhaps it is a parent or child, a priest or politician, terrorists or yourself — where is the need for forgiveness in your life?

#4 A New Kind of Wisdom: Jesus' Sermon on the Mount

When Lent starts late (e.g., in March), the extra Sundays just before Ash Wednesday allow us to hear readings from Matthew's account of the Sermon on the Mount, which we often miss. These passages, along with the other readings connected to them, both challenge and comfort us, inviting our prayerful pondering. This article aims to assist that prayer, focusing on the readings for the Seventh and Eighth Sundays in Ordinary Time (Cycle A). The reader may find it helpful to begin with the Scripture passages.[12]

The Sermon on the Mount serves as the keynote address in Matthew's gospel. We hear Jesus the teacher. For Matthew's community Jesus was Wisdom Incarnate, and much of the Sermon is rooted in the Jewish wisdom tradition. In this tradition, the questions continually asked were these: Is the life of wisdom and righteousness really worth the effort? Will God vindicate the just? Can one meet persecution and death with the hope that one's destiny is in God's hands? In the Sermon on the Mount, we hear

Jesus offering us ideals and insights into life in God's reign.

The first two readings for the Seventh Sunday in Ordinary Time introduce themes of love, respect, and sacredness. The Book of Leviticus offers a rich and positive perspective on the law as the way of following God faithfully. This Sunday's text, a tiny part of the Holiness Code, gives the command to love one's neighbor. The gospels present Jesus using this passage when asked about the greatest commandment (SEE MARK 12:28-34, LUKE 10:25-28, MATT 22:35-40). Of course, for Jesus, "neighbor" was much more inclusive, as surprisingly expressed in the Good Samaritan story (SEE LUKE 10:29-37).

Paul, in the second reading, presents genuine wisdom, reminding the Corinthians that their community is a temple of God because the Spirit dwells in it: "The temple of God is holy, and you are that temple"(1 COR 3:17). Paul tells the Corinthians (and now us) that indeed every person is sacred, a dwelling place of God's Spirit.

In the gospel passage Jesus dramatically pulls these convictions into focus, turning values, visions, and expectations upside down. Jesus teaches very countercultural wisdom, probably the most challenging in the entire Sermon: be nonviolent, love your enemies, pray for your persecutors.

As a beginning of a response, it would be important to reflect on what really are our wisdom sources. What grounds our lives and directs our everyday decisions? We ponder the Scriptures and gather for Eucharist, desiring to live our lives according to the gospel. But there is so much competition! From advertising and television, from movies and music and social media, from business and politics, we get so many contradictory messages about what is really important in life. We receive messages that value things over people, messages that promote individualism and consumerism. Throughout our societies we encounter structures and decisions that support authoritarian power rather than authentic leadership, structures and decisions that increase fear and alienation and in so many ways contradict the consistent ethic of life. And all these can subtly shape our day-to-day lives.

In this context of competition of basic values, we hear Jesus' message: Be nonviolent. An accurate interpretation of Jesus' examples (turn the left cheek, give both garments, walk an extra mile) helps us to understand that he is not preaching passivity. Walter Wink's marvelous explanation in *Engaging the Powers* shows how Jesus' directives help the oppressed seize the initiative to protest humiliation and institutionalized inequality, even when structural change is not possible.[13] Jesus encourages creative, nonviolent resistance that promotes human dignity. What a challenge! Our lives are saturated with violence — from cartoons to crime shows to foreign policy and even to some of our theology. The constant message is that violence saves. But Jesus urges us to break old patterns, to interrupt the cycle of violence, to be creatively nonviolent.

Love your enemies. An honest examination of consciousness might reveal just who our enemies are. Some religious or political figure? The boss? One of our parents? Myself? Jesus moves beyond his heritage that was expressed in Leviticus and calls us to love our neighbor and our enemies.

Pray for your persecutors. Jesus teaches us that such action best reflects *Abba* God, who sends rain not only on the just but also on the unjust, sunlight on the good and the bad. In faith, we come to understand that Jesus reveals more of what human beings can be because there is more to God than we think.[14] Here is a new kind of wisdom: pray for those who persecute you.

Jesus' vision of life in God's reign challenges our instinctive and common-sense responses to the many horrors and violence in our world. Jesus models for us compassion and justice, reconciliation and love. Jesus calls us to transformed and transforming actions that resist evil nonviolently and promote the flourishing of all life.

On the Eighth Sunday, Jesus helps us to respond to this call by affirming God's enduring love and by inviting our trust. The invitation, however, comes in the challenging situations of suffering and choice.

The first reading, a very brief passage from the Book of Isaiah, comes from the section (CHAPTERS 40-55) authored by an unknown prophet now simply called Second Isaiah. This prophet lived with the Israelite people in exile in Babylon in the mid 500s BCE (more than 150 years after the prophet Isaiah of Jerusalem). Second Isaiah speaks words of hope to a discouraged and suffering people.

Appropriately, the passage begins with lament. "But Zion said, 'The Lord has forsaken me; my Lord has forgotten me.'" Lament is a necessary and proper response to suffering, offering the first step to healing and giving voice to intolerable oppression. Lament is found throughout the Bible, including the very beginning of the exodus:

> After a long time the king of Egypt died. The Israelites groaned under their slavery, and cried out. Out of the slavery their cry for help rose up to God. God heard their groaning and God remembered the covenant ... and God took notice of them (EXOD 2:23-25).

Like the Hebrews in Egypt, Second Isaiah, and the people in Babylon, we too experience suffering and alienation in our personal, civic, and religious lives. We may even feel as though we are in exile: hurt, distrust, and separation in our family relationships; partisan bickering and posturing in politics; cover-ups and questions of credibility in religion. Illness, natural disasters, and polarization all around—how we need lament!

The Psalms show us how to speak out against such suffering and injustice, maybe even against God (SEE PSALM 88). Such crying out helps us to both grieve and grow into mature covenant partners with God. Lament allows us to stay in conversation with God, deepening the relationship and gradually moving to a new trust. Through the persons, prayer, and other events in our lives we too may hear in the depths of our hearts those gentle, loving words spoken through Second Isaiah: "I will never forget you."

Undoubtedly, Jesus must have had such an experience, grounding his intimate, loving relationship with *Abba* God. Throughout the gospels we catch glimpses of this profound relationship expressed in Jesus' words and deeds. This Sunday's passage from the Sermon on the Mount points to the deep trust that Jesus had in God and to Jesus' desire that others also experience this trust. There is also challenge: Jesus speaks to the choice we make concerning ultimate value in life. Where do we place our trust?

In the opening lines, Jesus is very direct: no one can serve two masters; no one can serve God and wealth. Ancient wisdom addresses contemporary challenges. We are overwhelmed with economic concerns, including worries about recession, debt crises, loss of homes and jobs, the number of people living in poverty. These are important issues. Jesus presses us to consider what is of ultimate value in the midst of these realities. Is mammon or God's loving presence the basis for all our behavior?

While the worldwide issues are of great significance for all humanity, especially the poorest who suffer most intensely, for many of us the more immediate challenge comes from living in a consumer society. Advertising preaches the market gospel. We turn things into people and people into things. In our societies, more possessions mean more happiness. Consumption becomes an addiction.

Jesus presents a different vision, cautioning about excessive worry concerning eating and drinking and clothing. In emphasizing proper priorities, Jesus is not discussing appropriate prudence and care. Rather he is stressing the wisdom of single heartedness and dependence on God, suggesting that our experience of ordinary things like birds and flowers can give us a new perception, a glimpse of God's enduring love. Do not worry; trust in God.

In these Sundays of Ordinary Time, Wisdom Incarnate offers us a challenging and comforting vision for our prayer. This new kind of wisdom calls us to nonviolence and love of enemies, rooted in a profound trust in God, a God who speaks tenderly to us: "I will never forget you."

ENDNOTES

1. These readings are Gen 2:18-24; Heb 2:9-11; Mark 10:2-16.
2. Karl Rahner, S.J., *The Practice of Faith* (New York: Crossroad, 1986) p. xi.
3. For example, see www.catholicclimatecovenant.org.
4. *God for Us: The Trinity and Christian Life* by Catherine Mowry LaCugna offers keen insight and wisdom.
5. The readings are 2 Sam 12:7-10, 13; Gal 2:16, 19-21; Luke 7:36-8:3. The reader may find it helpful to read these Scriptures first.
6. That forgiveness came before the anointing is emphasized in another transla-

tion of this verse: "her sins, many as they are, have been forgiven, as this out-pouring of her love shows" (Scholars Version).

7. "Can One Forgive a Child Molester?" by Stephen J. Pope in *America*, 18 Nov 2000, pp. 17-20.

8. Ibid., p. 18.

9. Ibid.

10. "No Peace Without Justice, No Justice Without Forgiveness," by Pope John Paul II, §8, 9. See www.vatican.va.

11. Ibid, §10.

12. The readings for the Seventh Sunday are: Lev 19:1-2, 17-18; 1Cor 3:16-23; Matt 5:38-48. For the Eighth Sunday: Is 49:14-15, 1Cor 4:4-15, Matt 6:24-34.

13. Walter Wink, *Engaging the Powers*, Minneapolis: Fortress Press, 1992, pp. 175-184.

14. Arthur Dewey, *The Word in Time* (revised edition), New Berlin, WI: Liturgical Publications, 1990, pp. 39-46.

CHAPTER 10

Poverty, Economics, and Justice

In recent years there has been talk about the bottom billion, even a book on the topic.[1] A harsh phrase, but a much harsher reality. Who are the bottom billion (whatever the exact number)? They are the women, men, and children who live in extreme poverty, without sufficient food, clean water, and other basic necessities of life.

Despite such staggering suffering, recent UN reports actually do offer some hope. Global initiatives have been effective in reducing the number of people living in extreme poverty. More children are participating in primary education. People suffering with AIDS or malaria are receiving more help.[2]

Still, many gains are being eroded by economic and financial crises, wars, and natural disasters. The poorest suffer the most. Gaps between the rich and the poor are increasing; hundred of millions of people struggle to survive on little income; every day thousands of children die due to poverty.[3] This litany could go on and on.

The Complexity of Poverty

Let one story symbolize millions.[4] Nsanga, a woman in her twenties with two children, had been married to a schoolteacher. Because of structural adjustment measures instituted by the International Monetary Fund (IMF), the government of Zaire (now the Democratic Republic of Congo) was forced to make cutbacks in its expenses, including laying off teachers and health workers. Nsanga's husband lost his job, was not able to find a new one, began spending their small resources on drinking, and finally simply disappeared.

Nsanga was very poor, as were her living conditions. She lived in a "single room which was part of a corrugated-roofed block surrounding an open courtyard. The yard contained a shared water tap, a roofless bathing stall, and a latrine, but no electricity.... Mosquitoes were ubiquitous in the neighborhood, and malaria and diarrheal diseases were common causes of death in young children. Many families ate only one meal per day and children were especially undernourished."[5]

Nsanga, like most poor women in Kinshasa (the capital city with a population of more than a million people at the time), had only a few years of education in primary school. She unsuccessfully tried to find employment and so performed small jobs in the neighborhood. These were not enough to pay for rent and food, so Nsanga began exchanging sex for subsistence. For a year, her lover was a married man who paid her rent. After she became pregnant, he left her, so Nsanga had to find more partners. At the time, the "neighborhood rate was equivalent to U.S. fifty cents per brief encounter,"[6] so two partners per day would produce about $30 a month.

Though experiencing the symptoms of AIDS, Nsanga was never tested. "Abandonment, divorce, and widowhood force many women who are without other resources into commercial sex work. In the presence of HIV, however, this survival strategy has been transformed into a death strategy."[7]

Nsanga's story points to the pervasive power of poverty. It also highlights the impact of socioeconomic and political conditions, including the consequences of IMF policies and the cultural oppression of women.

Clearly, the harsh realities of global poverty demand attention, but may also lead many people to wonder what individuals or small groups can do. The complex issues seem overwhelming. What can we do?

Unexamined Assumptions

First, we must ask ourselves what it is that we see and hear. We have heard the statistics and stories; we have seen the heartrending photos. But how do we filter those stories and photos? Do our own political and cultural values or some unexamined convictions color our perceptions and judgments?

The thought of Karl Rahner, S.J., on "global prescientific convictions" (discussed in Chapter One) also applies here.[8] These unexamined assumptions mold people's moral imaginations and perceptions of basic values, sometimes making it difficult to live gospel values. In other words, in some situations for some Christians, another set of values and convictions becomes more important than the gospel; for example, maximization of profits trumps solidarity and care for the poor.

So, our first step in answering "What can we do?" is the careful examination of the values and convictions that form the foundation of our perceptions and judgments. We may find that in some situations our gender or class or political party is more influential than the gospel — although we desire and even profess that our lives are rooted in the biblical tradition, especially the gospel.

A contemporary expression of this tradition can both help us refine and refocus our values and convictions and also inspire our concrete actions regarding global poverty: the U.S. bishops' pastoral letter, *Economic Justice for All*.

A Christian Vision

While many specific issues have changed since the letter was published in 1986 (globalization probably being the most significant), the basic perspective and convictions of the document remain relevant and challenging, offering insight and hope for responding to global poverty.

The letter claims that economic life is one of the chief areas where people live out their faith, love their neighbor, and fulfill God's creative design.[9] Economic decisions affect the quality of people's lives, even to the point of determining whether people live or die (as we saw in Nsanga's story).

In response to massive problems of homelessness, unemployment, poverty, and starvation, the bishops offer a Christian vision of the economic life. The basic criterion against which all aspects of economic life must be measured is the dignity of the person along with the community and solidarity that are essential to this dignity. *Economic Justice for All* first turns to the Scriptures for developing the specifics of this sacredness of human beings, and then spells out familiar social justice themes of rights, duties, and the common good.

In developing the biblical theme of discipleship, *Economic Justice for All* explains the contemporary phrase, "preferential option for the poor." The bishops point out that in the New Testament salvation is extended to all people. At the same time, Jesus takes the side of those most in need, physically and spiritually. Contemporary followers of Jesus, then, are challenged to take on this perspective: to see things from the side of the poor, to assess lifestyle and public policies in terms of their impact on the poor, to experience God's power in the midst of poverty and powerlessness.[10]

Following the tradition of Catholic social teaching, *Economic Justice for All* considers the global economy from the perspective of human dignity, justice, and the common good. Although the social teaching does not demand absolute equality of wealth, it does challenge the shocking inequality between the rich and the poor.

Because of its wealth and power, the United States has a primary role in reforming the international economic order, particularly in relation to the developing world. It must work with other influential nations, with multilateral institutions, and with transnational banks and corporations. *Economic Justice for All* reviews five major areas where reform is needed and possible: 1) development assistance through grants, low-interest loans, and technical aid; 2) trade policy that is especially sensitive to the poorest nations; 3) international finance and investment, with special attention to the debt crisis of developing nations; 4) private investment in foreign countries; 5) an international food system that increases immediate food aid and develops long-term programs to combat hunger.[11] (Action steps for ordinary people will be discussed below.)

This critique of capitalism (also expressed by John Paul II in his writings, especially *On Social Concern* and *On the Hundredth Anniversary of Rerum Novarum,* and by Benedict XVI in *Charity in Truth*) may surprise many people in the developed world. Perhaps without even being aware of it, these people have internalized the market values of their society.[12] Gospel values, as developed and applied by the social teachings, may seem idealistic and out of touch with reality — or simply be rejected as some form of communism or socialism. *Economic Justice for All* and the papal encyclicals, then, offer serious content for the prayerful examination of our convictions and our follow-up actions.

What Can We Do?

So, what are some action steps for ordinary people? *Economic Justice for All* was developed to offer moral guidance including, in part, participation in shaping public policy. Political policies and economic structures provide the means to address global poverty by creating a societal environment that promotes the flourishing of life. Trade agreements, aid to developing nations, political relations and tensions, climate change all deserve careful attention. In the domestic scene, there is need for more jobs with adequate pay and decent working conditions, for immigration reform, for continued healthcare reform, for improved education. Clearly then, how we vote, the advocacy groups we support, our own involvement through letters to elected officials, the values our churches and schools and families teach and embody — all these are ordinary but real action steps we can take to address global poverty in the spirit of the gospel as expressed in the pastoral letter.

Some direct experience of poverty expands our horizons and allows us to encounter real people and real poverty. Many different possibilities are available. Here are just a few examples: at home, working with St. Vincent de Paul groups; volunteering at a Catholic Worker house, food pantry, or homeless shelter; beyond our borders, participating in an immersion experience in the developing world instead of a tourist vacation; developing a plan to spend several years living and working among the extremely poor; as a bridge between home and beyond, sponsoring a child and developing a relationship with the family; a parish program that supports micro-financing projects in the developing world.[13]

In preparation for all these action steps (or as a response to them), we need to search out accurate information, recognizing that some information may be influenced by values contrary to the gospel. We try to pay attention to trustworthy sources, especially those working directly with the poor.

For example, in the debate about trade agreements we heard many positive things in the media from corporations and government about neoliberal globalization. This view stresses privatization, decreased regulation by governments, the lowering of barriers to international trade. The Jesuit superiors of Latin America offered a different view, rooted in their actual experience and in their commitment to the Church's social teachings. They list some of the destructive results of neoliberal globalization: "the immense imbalances and perturbations neoliberalism causes through the concentration of income, wealth and land ownership; the multiplication of the unemployed urban masses or those surviving in unstable and unproductive jobs; ... the destruction and forced displacement of indigenous and peasant populations; ... the disappearance of food security; and increase in criminality often triggered by hunger."[14] Especially for those of us who have not experienced extreme poverty first-hand, such testimony is invaluable for the formation of our consciences.

As we consider what we can do, we need to be realistic in what we are *able* to do; we need to be honest in what we *ought* to do. No individual or group can pursue all issues, but they can do something; and in doing that one thing they must respect all life.

Scripture scholar Walter Wink expresses a similar insight in terms of vocation, urging us "to seek the specific shape of our own divine calling in the day-to-day working out of our relationship with God." He explains, "We are not called to do everything, to heal everything, to change everything, but only to do what God asks of us. And in the asking is supplied the power to perform it. We are freed from the paralysis that results from being overwhelmed by the immensity of the need and our relative powerlessness, and we are freed from messianic megalomania, in which we try to heal everyone that hurts."[15] However, we can and must do something.

We ought not underestimate the challenge of being pro-life in the full sense of the term. In his encyclical *The Gospel of Life* Pope John Paul II urged all persons to choose life—consistently, personally, nationally, globally.[16] This invitation is really a profound challenge: to look deeply into ourselves and to test against the gospel some of our own deeply held beliefs and practices and then to act.

There is much to do, much that we can do. Even as we begin to discern our unexamined assumptions and to enter into the realities of global poverty, an appropriate first response is lament. *Be gracious to us, O God. Enter our lament in your book. Store every tear in your flask* (SEE PSALM 56). More words of wisdom from Walter Wink:

> We are so interconnected with all of life that we cannot help being touched by the pain of all that suffers. ... We human beings are far too frail and tiny to bear all this pain. ... What we need is a portable form of the Wailing Wall in Jerusalem, where we can unburden ourselves of this accumulated suffering. We need to experience it; it is a part of reality. ... But we must not try to bear the suffer-

ings of the creation ourselves. We are to articulate these agonizing longings and let them pass through us to God. Only the heart at the center of the universe can endure such a weight of suffering.[17]

Lament helps us to speak out against suffering and oppression, ultimately renewing and deepening our relationship with God. Lament is also necessary for life in society, raising questions of power and calling for change in unjust situations.[18] Lament is an appropriately human and a profoundly religious response to global poverty.

Lament leads to action. We have considered the inspired vision of *Economic Justice for All*, guiding our action steps. *This is the fast that I wish: untying the thongs of the yoke, sharing your bread, not turning your back* (SEE ISAIAH 58:5-7). Following the prophets and Jesus, we discern the implications of our vocation, including the specific means of criticizing and changing oppressive structures and of energizing people's hopes and actions.[19]

People of faith can work with many others, searching in solidarity for creative and courageous ways to overcome poverty and its causes. People of faith also bring their own particular motivation and vision, rooted in their religious beliefs. Ultimately, Christians can face suffering and political and economic challenges and take action because they trust in God. *Do not let your hearts be troubled; trust in God* (SEE JOHN 14:1). This is not a pie-in-the-sky optimism, but a profound conviction about the God revealed by Jesus.[20] This God suffers with us, leads us as individuals and as community in resisting evil, and brings us all to the fullness of life.

Awareness, lament, action, trust — we can do this for justice and life for the bottom billion and all God's creation!

ENDNOTES

1. Paul Collier, *The Bottom Billion* (New York: Oxford University Press, 2007).

2. The Millennium Development Goals Reports, United Nations, www.un.org/millenniumgoals/reports.shtml.

3. Catholics Confront Global Poverty, www.crs.org; see also www.globalissues.org.

4. Nsanga's story is taken from Brooke Grundfest Schoepf, "Health, Gender Relations, and Poverty in the AIDS Era," in *Courtyards, Markets, City Streets: Urban Women in Africa*, ed. Kathleen Sheldon (Boulder, Colo.: Westview Press, 1996), 153-168. Though somewhat dated, Nsanga's story still accurately describes today's realities.

5. Ibid., 157-58.

6. Ibid., 159.

7. Ibid., 160.

8. Karl Rahner, S.J., "On Bad Arguments in Moral Theology," *Theological Investigations* vol. XVIII (New York: Crossroad, 1983), 74-85.

9. National Conference of Catholic Bishops, *Economic Justice for All : Pastoral Letter*

on *Catholic Social Teaching and the U.S. Economy*, (Washington, DC: USCC Office of Publishing, 1986), §6 in Pastoral Message.

10. Ibid., §§ 48-52.

11. Ibid., §§ 261-294.

12. An example of an "unexamined assumption" mentioned earlier; also see John Kavanaugh, *Following Christ in a Consumer Society*, 25th anniversary edition (Maryknoll: Orbis Books, 2006).

13. See, for example, www.kiva.org.

14. Jesuit Provincials of Latin America, "For Life and Against Neoliberalism," in *We Make the Road by Walking: Central America, Mexico, and the Caribbean in the New Millennium*, eds. Ann Butwell, Kathy Ogle, and Scott Wright (Washington, DC: EPICA, 1998), 76. For another excellent example, see Peter Henriot's article in *Forum* (Summer 2010), "Reading the Signs of the Times in Our Globalized World: the Challenge from Africa." For a careful study of the issues, see John Sniegocki, *Catholic Social Teaching and Economic Globalization* (Milwaukee: Marquette University Press, 2009).

15. Walter Wink, *Engaging the Powers* (Minneapolis: Fortress Press, 1992), 307.

16. John Paul II, *The Gospel of Life* (Boston: Pauline Books and Media, 1995), #98-#101.

17. Wink, *Powers*, 305.

18. Walter Brueggemann, "The Costly Loss of Lament," *Journal for the Study of the Old Testament*, vol. 36 (1986): 62-64.

19. Walter Brueggemann, *The Prophetic Imagination*, second edition (Minneapolis: Fortress Press, 2001), especially 39-79.

20. Arthur J. Dewey, *The Word in Time* revised edition (New Berlin, Wis: Liturgical Publications, 1990), 31 and passim. See also Francis J. Molony, S.D.B., *The Gospel of John* (Collegeville: The Liturgical Press, 1998) and J. Massynberde Ford, *Redeemer: Friend and Mother* (Minneapolis: Fortress Press, 1997).

CHAPTER 11

The Death Penalty

Why the Church Speaks a Countercultural Message

If someone murdered your child or closest friend, what punishment would you want for the criminal? If you were simply asked your opinion about capital punishment, how would you respond? What reasons would you give for your answer?

Recent polls show that 63 percent of U.S. citizens favor the death penalty. Yet the U.S. Catholic bishops, along with many other religious leaders, have spoken out *against* capital punishment. Beyond polls and statements, powerful scenes dramatize opposing viewpoints: people protesting a death sentence with candlelight vigils while others gather as if at a party shouting, "Kill the scum!"

This chapter considers these profound differences in our society, summarizes the teaching of the U.S. bishops, and tells a mother's true story of horror and reconciliation after the murder of her daughter.

Conflicting Public Opinions

In 1966, less than half of the U.S. population approved of the death penalty. Now polls indicate that over 60 percent approve. Why this dramatic change in public opinion? Certainly, a major factor is the increasing fear and frustration concerning violent crime. Something must be done! Many people turn to the death penalty as a possible remedy. Not only has the public turned in favor of capital punishment, but the U.S. government has also recommended that many more crimes be punishable by the death penalty. This renewed approval reflects traditional reasons for supporting the death penalty: deterrence and retribution. Some who support capital punishment do so because they judge that the threat of death will prevent people from committing crimes. Others judge that some crimes are so horrible that the only appropriate punishment is death.

Those people who oppose the death penalty, however, challenge these traditional reasons. They point out that there is no solid evidence that the death penalty serves as a deterrent. Indeed, they note, examples point in the opposite direction: Some countries that have eliminated the death penalty have had decreasing rates of violent crime, and some death-penalty states have had increasing rates of homicide. Supporters of capital punishment counter with the argument that the death penalty would be more effective as a deterrent were it not for the many appeals, long delays, and limited numbers of those actually executed.

Similar debates surround the issue of retribution. Opponents of capital punishment claim that there is no place in a civilized society for justifying death in terms of retribution. They judge such action to be closer to sheer revenge. They doubt that death can be a means of balancing the disturbed equilibrium of justice that resulted from the original crime. Again, supporters counter with the claim that society will not respect the law unless society's sense of justice is satisfied by the criminal's death.

Other supporters claim that retribution is self-justifying, simply a return in kind. Some justify retribution by appealing to the Bible: "[Y]ou shall give life for life, eye for eye, tooth for tooth..." (EXODUS 21:23, 24). Scripture scholars tell us that the eye-for-eye mandate is actually an attempt to limit violence in early Hebrew culture. As we know from experience, violence tends to escalate: If you cut off my finger, I retaliate by cutting off your hand. Eye-for-eye reduced such escalation. As we will see later in this article, eye-for-eye must be considered in the context of the whole Bible.

Many people have made up their minds about the death penalty without really thinking out its moral implications. They then find and use studies, statistics, and stories to fit their conclusions. Could this be true for you? If so, you—and all who are willing to wrestle with this issue—will have to look behind the convictions and be open to developing a new attitude. One's gut-level response may be very strong, but it doesn't necessarily lead to good moral decisions.

Teaching of the U.S. Bishops

The Catholic bishops of the United States have provided careful guidance about this difficult issue, applying the teaching of the universal Church to our American culture. Along with the leadership assemblies of many Churches (for example, American Baptists, Disciples of Christ, Episcopalians, Lutherans, Presbyterians), the U.S. bishops have expressed their opposition to the death penalty. First articulated in 1974, the bishops' position is explained in a 1980 statement, *Capital Punishment*. Individual bishops and state conferences of bishops have repeated in numerous teachings their opposition to the death penalty.

In their 1980 statement, the bishops begin by noting that punishment, "since it involves the deliberate infliction of evil on another," must be justifiable. They acknowledge that the Christian tradition has for a long time recognized a government's right to protect its citizens by using the death penalty in some serious situations. The bishops ask, however, whether capital punishment is still justifiable in the present circumstances in the United States.

In this context, the bishops enter the debate about deterrence and retribution. They acknowledge that capital punishment certainly prevents the criminal from committing more crimes, yet question whether it prevents others from doing so. Similarly, concerning retribution, the bishops support the arguments against death as an appropriate form of punishment. The bishops add that reform is a third reason given to justify punishment, but it clearly does not apply in the case of capital punishment. And so they affirm: "We believe that in the conditions of contemporary American society, the legitimate purposes of punishment do not justify the imposition of the death penalty."

The Heart of the Matter

As with the debate in our wider society, it is important to move behind the discussion of deterrence and retribution to get to the heart of the bishops' position. The statement does just that, by discussing four related values that would be promoted by the abolition of the death penalty.

First, "abolition sends a message that we can break the cycle of violence, that we need not take life for life, that we can envisage more humane and more hopeful and effective responses to the growth of violent crime." The bishops recognize that crime is rooted in the complex reality of contemporary society, including those "social conditions of poverty and injustice which often provide the breeding grounds for serious crime." More attention should go to correcting the root causes of crime than to enlarging death row.

Second, "abolition of capital punishment is also a manifestation of our belief in the unique worth and dignity of each person from the moment of conception, a creature made in the image and likeness of God." This belief, rooted in Scripture and consistently expressed in the social teachings of the Church, applies to all people, including those who have taken life.

Third, "abolition of the death penalty is further testimony to our conviction, a conviction which we share with the Judaic and Islamic traditions, that God is indeed the Lord of life." And so human life in all its stages is sacred, and human beings are called to care for life, that is, to exercise good stewardship and not absolute control. The bishops recognize that abortion, euthanasia, and the death penalty are not the same issue, but they each point to the same fundamental value: safeguarding the sanctity of life.

Fourth, "we believe that abolition of the death penalty is most consonant with the example of Jesus." In many ways, this final point summarizes the other three: the God revealed in the life of Jesus is a God of forgiveness and redemption, of love and compassion—in a word, a God of life. The heart of the bishops' position on the death penalty, then, is found in the gospel.

Gut-level reactions may cry out for vengeance, but Jesus' example in the gospels invites all to develop a new and different attitude toward violence. The bishops encourage us to embody Jesus' message in practical and civic decisions.

Prisons, Victims, and More

While the gospel leads the bishops to oppose the death penalty, they also recognize the need that society has to protect itself. Imprisonment will be necessary but ought not to dehumanize the convicts. The bishops summarize what they have developed in other documents: significant changes in the prison system are necessary to make it truly conducive to reform and rehabilitation.

In their statement on capital punishment, the bishops express special concern for the victims of violent crime and their families. "Our society should not flinch from contemplating the suffering that violent crime brings to so many when it destroys lives, shatters families and crushes the hope of the innocent." Care for victims must be given in practical ways, such as financial assistance, pastoral care, medical and psychological treatment.

Some other difficulties directly related to the death penalty, which the statement mentions, are (1) the death penalty removes the possibility of reform and rehabilitation, (2) there is the possibility of putting an innocent person to death, (3) carrying out the death penalty causes anguish not only for the convict's loved ones but also for the executioners and the witnesses, (4) executions attract great publicity, much of it unhealthy, (5) there is legitimate concern that criminals are sentenced to death in a discriminatory way: "It is a reasonable judgment that racist attitudes and the social consequences of racism have some influence in determining who is sentenced to die in our society." Adequate legal representation is an issue that puts poor people at a disadvantage. For many reasons, especially the message of Jesus, the U.S. bishops favor ending the death penalty.

Scripture and Tradition

The Bible is often mentioned in debates about the death penalty. Supporters quote the Exodus passage, eye for eye, while opponents appeal to Ezekiel (33:11): "As I live, says the Lord God, I swear I take no pleasure in the death of the wicked man, but rather in the wicked man's conversion, that he may live." In fact, such use of the Bible (finding a "proof text" to affirm one's point of view) is inappropriate.

Scripture scholars teach us to understand the Bible (and its individual books) in historical context: when it was written and why. Thus considered, there is ambivalence about capital punishment in the Scriptures.

Clearly, the Hebrew Scriptures allowed the death penalty (for a much longer list of offenses than our society would be comfortable with—for example, striking or cursing a parent, adultery, idolatry). Yet, as we see in Ezekiel and many other passages, there is also an attempt to limit violence and to stress mercy. In the Christian Scriptures, Jesus' life and teachings (SEE THE SERMON ON THE MOUNT, MATT 5:1–7:29) focus on mercy, reconciliation, and redemption. (It may also be instructive to recall that Jesus' death was itself an application of the death penalty.) The basic thrust of the gospels supports opposition to the death penalty.

Indeed, the early Church (for example, in the writings of Clement of Rome [d. 101] and Justin Martyr [d. 165]) generally found taking human life to be incompatible with the gospel. Christians were not to participate in capital punishment. Later, after Christianity became the religion of the Roman Empire, opposition to the death penalty declined. Augustine recognized the death penalty as a means of deterring the wicked and protecting the innocent. In the Middle Ages, Thomas Aquinas reaffirmed this position.

The *Catechism of the Catholic Church* reflects this tradition, stating that the death penalty is possible in cases of extreme gravity. The *Catechism* adds that means other than killing should be preferred when these would be sufficient to protect public order (§2267). Saint Pope John Paul II expressed a stronger position against the death penalty in his encyclical *The Gospel of Life*. He stressed that situations where its use is necessary to protect society have become "very rare, if not practically nonexistent" (56). When visiting the United States in 1999, John Paul called the death penalty "cruel and unnecessary" and affirmed that the "dignity of human life must never be taken away, even in the case of someone who has done great evil."

A Mother's Story

Despite the message of Jesus and the teachings of the bishops, many people may still be caught up in the anger and outrage over violent crime. Scriptures and teachings seem so remote; debates over deterrence and retribution prove nothing. For all, but especially for those who feel this way, the following true story may be especially challenging.

Marietta Jaeger and her family were on a camping vacation in Montana when her seven-year-old daughter, Susie, was kidnapped. Searches by the FBI and local authorities turned up nothing. Jaeger describes her initial feelings about the kidnapper: "I could kill him. I meant it with every fiber of my being. I'm sure I could have done it with my bare hands and a smile on my face. I felt it was a matter of justice."

Months passed with no new clues, except a few calls from the kidnapper offering to exchange Susie for a ransom — but the kidnapper never made a specific offer. During this time Jaeger "argued and argued with God," and then "gave God permission to change my heart." Jaeger also began to pray for the kidnapper, acknowledging that "my Christian upbringing and my knowledge of good psychological health had taught me that forgiveness was not an option, but a mandate."

Fifteen months after Susie's kidnapping, the kidnapper was arrested. Although the death penalty was applicable in the case, Jaeger asked the FBI to settle for the alternative—life imprisonment with psychiatric care. Only then did the kidnapper, a young man, finally admit to the rape, strangulation death, decapitation, and dismemberment of Susie (within a week of the kidnapping). A short time later, the young man committed suicide.

Jaeger recognizes the need for society to protect itself. "I do not advocate forgiveness for violent people and then release to the streets. I know that there are people who should be separated in a humanely secured manner from the community for the protection of all."

And, of course, she knows intimately the feelings of the victim's family. She understands the desire for revenge but claims that those who retain an attitude of vindictiveness are tormented, embittered people who have no peace of mind. The quality of their lives is diminished, and, in effect, they have given the offender another victim. Jaeger states that the death penalty does not do for the victims' family what they had hoped but leaves them "empty, unsatisfied, and unhealed." She adds, "There is no number of retaliatory deaths which would compensate to me the inestimable value of my daughter's life, nor would they restore her to my arms."

Consistent Ethic of Life

Marietta Jaeger's story is a striking embodiment of Jesus' message and the bishops' recent teachings. Her life—and the lives of so many others like her—is also a dramatic reminder that the ideal can be lived in the real world. Much in our culture—fears, political platforms, media events—promotes a different message. Jaeger's witness, however, challenges all of us to move beyond brutalization to develop a consistent ethic of life, to appreciate the sanctity of all life. Concrete steps can include such activities as study groups, prayer services, letter-writing to state and federal legislators, addressing the root causes of crime in our society, and contacting groups such as Murder Victims' Families for Reconciliation.

But it all starts with developing a new attitude about violence, an attitude rooted in the countercultural message of the gospel.

CHAPTER 12

HIV/AIDS

What Can We Do?

Despite the fact that more than half of those estimated to be infected with HIV do not know they are infected, there has been a sharp decline in public concern regarding HIV and AIDS. World AIDS Day, December 1, provides us an opportunity for renewed awareness and action. So does every other day!

Recent UN reports do offer some hope. Global initiatives, including the Global Fund to Fight AIDS, Tuberculosis, and Malaria (GFATM) and the U.S. President's Emergency Plan for AIDS Relief (PEPFAR), are providing antiretroviral medications to millions of infected persons.

Still, many do not have access to these medications. Money for treatment has stopped growing. Because of drug shortages, clinics may have to turn people away. Around the world, thousands of people become newly infected every day.

Harsh realities—millions infected or already deceased, staggering suffering, economic structures that along with war and oppression of women promote the spread of HIV—demand attention, but may also lead many people to wonder what individuals or small groups can do. The complex issues seem overwhelming. What can we do?

We find wise guidance for a response in human rights and various religious traditions. A Christian expression of this wisdom, rooted in the biblical tradition and a contemporary expression of it, the consistent ethic of life, suggests a three-part process for caring for one another: lament, act, and discern links.

Because the epidemic causes intense suffering, the first part of responding is lament. In his book *Engaging the Powers*, Scripture scholar Walter Wink offers these words of wisdom.

> We are so interconnected with all of life that we cannot help being touched by the pain of all that suffers. ... We human beings are far too frail and tiny to bear all this pain. ... What we need is a portable form of the Wailing Wall in Jerusalem, where we can unburden ourselves of this accumulated suffering. We need to experience it; it is

a part of reality. ... But we must not try to bear the sufferings of the creation ourselves. We are to articulate these agonizing longings and let them pass through us to God. Only the heart at the center of the universe can endure such a weight of suffering.[1]

Lament helps us to speak out against suffering and oppression, ultimately renewing and deepening our relationship with God, as shown in a special way in the Psalms. Let's listen for a moment to Psalm 22: "My God, my God, why have you abandoned me? Why so far from my call for help, from my cries of anguish? ... Yet you are enthroned as the Holy One.... In you our ancestors trusted; they trusted and you rescued them."

Lament is also necessary for life in society, raising questions of power and calling for change in unjust situations.[2] Lament is an appropriately human and a profoundly religious response to HIV and AIDS.

Lament inspires action. The second part of responding to the challenge and suffering found in the pandemic requires realism and honesty. We need to be realistic in what we can do; we need to be honest in what we ought to do. Again Walter Wink offers some helpful advice, urging us "to seek the specific shape of our own divine calling in the day-to-day working out of our relationship with God." He explains:

> We are not called to do everything, to heal everything, to change everything, but only to do what God asks of us. And in the asking is supplied the power to perform it. We are freed from the paralysis that results from being overwhelmed by the immensity of the need and our relative powerlessness, and we are freed from messianic megalomania, in which we try to heal everyone that hurts.[3]

Cardinal Joseph Bernardin, the late archbishop of Chicago, expressed a similar insight in his many talks on the consistent ethic of life. He affirmed that no individual or group can pursue all issues, but they can do something; and in doing that one thing they must respect all life. We are called not to do everything but only what God asks of us, from direct help in another country to a parish support group.

We also need to be honest as we confront the many ethical issues raised by HIV and AIDS, as we ask what ought we to do? This honesty will lead us to do the hard homework of examining our conscience, returning to the foundations of our Christian faith for a vision of the meaning of life. Our searching also considers the medical, social, economic, and political dimensions of each dilemma raised by the reality of HIV/AIDS.

Conscience does not make the action right or wrong; rather it recognizes the action as right or wrong. The rightness/wrongness is given in the total combination of act, intention, circumstances, consequences — does this promote human flourishing or undermine it? This emphasis on reality as the basis of morality opposes relativism. Thus, Cardinal Bernardin counsels us to remember that we encounter an "objective, albeit imperfectly perceived, moral order."[4]

The second part of our response to the many issues of the pandemic, then, is action rooted in realism and honesty, or using other words, vocation and conscience.

The third and final part is discerning links. Even as we focus on a particular problem, we desire to be aware of the relatedness of all life. Cardinal Bernardin consistently kept a balance in his views, acknowledging that issues are distinct and different yet always linked. "When human life is considered 'cheap' or easily expendable in one area," he wrote, "eventually nothing is held as sacred and all lives are in jeopardy."[5] Our passion for one issue concerning HIV/AIDS does not allow us to be insensitive to other moral claims or to contradict other life-respecting and life-saving practices.

The consistent ethic of life urges us to appreciate especially the complex, interwoven nature of the structural issues. The vicious cycles of unjust economic policies, war, poverty, and oppression of women contribute to the spread of HIV and cause dehumanization and death.[6] Understanding these links is as important as it is challenging, leading perhaps to another cycle of lament and action.

Lament, action, discerning links. In some ways this three-part response seems so simple—and yet our experience often reveals apathy, ignorance, and opposition. Situations, both local and global, seem overwhelming. So reflecting on the context of our lives raises important questions. What sustains the many cycles of our lament, action, and linkage? What keeps us going? What can we share with others?

As we confront the pandemic, whether in the virus itself or in our work and ministry or in our classes and research or in local and national conferences, we hear bad news and good news. The bad news: sobering statistics concerning the face of AIDS today, urgent problems in various places yet still an unjust distribution of resources, startling stigma from those who call themselves religious, the effects of a devastating recession including insufficient donations to meet growing needs.

The good news: millions of people are now receiving medications, the rates of infection are decreasing for some, renewed commitment to PEPFAR and the Global Fund has been promoted and new campaigns to increase awareness initiated, religious institutions are responding in many and varied ways to people in need.

Bad news. Good news. Two words may emerge in our consciousness as we experience this mix of news, as we ponder the dense complexity of the AIDS pandemic: "overwhelming" and "hope."

"Overwhelming" is almost always in a challenging, even negative, context. How can we possibly comprehend the reality of millions of infections from HIV/AIDS? Overwhelming. How do we change the deeply rooted pattern of stigma and discrimination? Overwhelming. What about the continuing prejudice toward our religious institutions, despite their record of compassionate care and service? Overwhelming. Even medical knowledge and breakthroughs seem overwhelming—what gifted and learned people grasp seemingly so easily staggers our minds and imaginations. Similarly, the complexity of the social, cultural, political, and economic structures—local and global—that drive the epidemic. Overwhelming. The number of people lost to AIDS—overwhelming.

But we also hear positive news. Signs of hope in the midst of the pandemic are noted again and again: new treatments, new money, creativity in our ministries, day-by-day commitment. The fundamental goodness and dignity of humanity offer us renewed promise. Worship reminds many of us that in every age God has been our hope.

Overwhelming. Hope. Jesus of Nazareth offers a way to transform these two opposite words into one energizing phrase: **overwhelming hope!**

Let's listen to one of his parables. "Again Jesus said, 'To what shall I compare the kingdom of God? It is like yeast that a woman took and mixed in with three measures of wheat flour until the whole batch of dough was leavened'" (LUKE 13:20-21).

Rooted in his profound experience of Abba God, Jesus used everyday stories to try to communicate that experience to his listeners, often with a surprising twist! What was everyday for his listeners may not be so for us. In this parable, for example, most of us do not know what three measures of flour means (we probably think three cups), and so we may miss Jesus' message. Generally in this parable, we focus on the leaven, not realizing that three measures of flour is enough for fifty pounds of bread![7] Fifty pounds of bread coming out of a little earthen oven. This is a glimpse of the reign of God, full of surprise and overflowing goodness. In the context of the AIDS pandemic, the parable can speak to us of overwhelming hope!

There is an old *I Love Lucy* television show (the episode is called "Pioneer Women") in which Lucy is baking bread. Suddenly the oven door pops open and a huge, many-feet-long loaf pours out. That is the parable. The reign of God—God's loving presence in our midst now—is overwhelming hope and joy and goodness.

In no way does Jesus' vision deny the pain and suffering and death because of HIV and AIDS; lament remains essential. It does not deny apathy and numbness; action remains essential. It does not deny alienation and ideology; discerning links remains essential. This hopeful vision does deny that suffering and death and apathy and alienation are the final word.

In our difficult times, perhaps we can remember this parable of the baker lady with her huge amount of bread. Perhaps we will even recall with some delight the image of Lucy. Jesus shares his conviction about Abba God's overflowing and surprising love, grounding our hope. This does not remove the darkness and doubt, but may keep it from tumbling into despair. Overwhelming hope sustains and enlivens our lament, action, and linkage.

Jesus proclaimed that God's loving presence can be experienced in the midst of ordinary life. This reign of God was different from the empire of Rome that dominated Jesus' homeland. God's empire is characterized by compassion and healing, trust and forgiveness, nonviolence and joy, love—yes, even love of enemies. Indeed, God entrusts us to one another. What can we do concerning HIV/AIDS? We can find time for reflection and prayer. We can renew our own commitment. We can recognize the importance of sharing with others our knowledge, concern, and vision. We can choose one concrete step to help stop AIDS.[8]

In the midst of apathy, suffering, discrimination and other ethical dilemmas, we still find energy, solidarity, and insight. As we confront the AIDS epidemic, we lament and act and discern links. In pastoral ministry and medical clinics, in education and policy-making, and in an extraordinary variety of other ways, we embrace and express our unique form of caring for one another. And all this in the context of overwhelming hope!

ENDNOTES

1. Walter Wink, *Engaging the Powers*, Minneapolis: Fortress Press, 1992, p. 305.
2. Walter Brueggemann, "The Costly Loss of Lament," *Journal for the Study of the Old Testament*, vol.36, 1986, pp. 62-64.
3. Wink, *Engaging*, p. 307.
4. Joseph Cardinal Bernardin, *A Moral Vision for America*, Washington, D.C.: Georgetown University Press, 1998, p. 111.
5. Joseph Cardinal Bernardin, *Consistent Ethic of Life*, Kansas City: Sheed & Ward, 1988, p. 89.
6. See Kenneth R. Overberg, S.J., *Ethics and AIDS: Compassion and Justice in Global Crisis*, Lanham: Rowman & Littlefield Publishers, 2006, pp. 73-134.
7. Alan Culpepper, "The Gospel of Luke," *The New Interpreter's Bible*, Nashville: Abingdon Press, 1995, vol. nine, p. 276.
8. For basic facts about HIV and AIDS and much other information, see www.avert.org.

CHAPTER 13

The Mystery of God and Suffering

Suffering surrounds us, from broken families to earthquakes, from poverty to torture, from cancer to starvation. Such personal and global anguish often leads people to ask about God: "Who is God?" "How can a good and gracious God allow this to happen?" "Where is God in all this suffering?" "Is there a God?" Those directly involved in suffering often ask: "Why did this happen to me?" and sometimes even "What did I do wrong to be punished in this way?"

Humans have long searched for satisfying insights into these and similar questions. The whole Book of Job in the Bible is dedicated to this topic. Christians have focused, in particular, on the suffering and death of Jesus in the hope of discovering meaning for suffering. Some of these biblical perspectives, however, fail to satisfy contemporary hearts and minds that long for the compassionate God revealed by Jesus.

In order to penetrate more deeply into the mystery of God and suffering and to develop an understanding closer to the vision of Jesus, we first consider the life and death of Jesus, including some of the prominent interpretations of his suffering and death. We will then return to Scripture and the tradition for another perspective on Jesus' life and death. We will discover what this view means for our image of God and how it grounds a threefold response to suffering of lament, action, and trust.

Jesus' Life and Teachings

From the Gospels, we learn three important points about Jesus and suffering: 1) Jesus resisted suffering and its personal and social causes and is frequently described healing the sick; 2) Jesus rejected the conviction that suffering is the punishment for sin; 3) Jesus expressed a profound trust in a loving, compassionate, and present God.

First, Mark's Gospel (1:40-42) describes an encounter between Jesus and a leper. With a simple but profound touch, Jesus heals the leper, breaks down barriers, challenges purity laws that alienate, and embodies his convictions about the inclusive meaning of the reign of God.[1] This event reveals not only Jesus' care for an individual in need but also his concern about structures of society that oppress people.

Second, deeply embedded in some streams of Hebrew thought is the conviction (called the Law of Retribution) that good deeds lead to blessing and evil deeds to suffering. If a person were experiencing sickness or other trials, then that person must have sinned in the past.[2] The Hebrew people in exile in Babylon, for example, interpreted this political-social event as God's punishment for their failure to follow the covenant faithfully. This conviction appears in many religions and cultures. Jesus, however, rejected it. Matthew's Jesus in the Sermon on the Mount describes God as showering rain on evil persons as well as good ones (MATT 5:45). Similarly, John's Jesus heals the blind man and explicitly rejects the idea that suffering is punishment for sin (JOHN 9:1-41, ESPECIALLY 2-5).

Third, implicitly and explicitly the gospels reveal Jesus' intimate, loving relationship with God. Jesus' surprising use of *Abba* to describe God conveys a sense of simplicity, familiarity, fidelity and trust.[3] The parables also give us a glimpse of Jesus' sense of God. The Prodigal Son (LUKE 15:11-32) tells us a lot about the father who forgives the son without any bitterness, celebrates his return, and consoles the angry older brother. *Abba* is a loving, forgiving, gentle parent. Even as he faced suffering and death, Jesus remained faithful to his call, always trusting God. In the Resurrection, God confirms Jesus' faithfulness.

Interpreting a Terrible Death

The life and teaching of Jesus highlighted the healing presence of a God of love and life. In the end, however, Jesus suffered a horrible execution. Death, first Jesus' and later others', led the early Christian communities to search for meaning. In light of their experience of the risen Jesus, they looked to their culture and their Hebrew Scriptures for possible interpretations. They included these insights in their preaching and eventually in the Christian Scriptures.

From culture they knew about ransom. From their Jewish rituals they also understood sacrifice and atonement. From their Wisdom literature they were familiar with the theme of the vindication of the Innocent Sufferer (SEE WISDOM 2:17-20 AND 5:5, 15-16; ALSO 2 MACC 7, AND DAN 6). From the prophet Isaiah (CHAPTERS 42, 49, 50, 52-53) Jesus' followers creatively used the songs of the Suffering Servant to interpret Jesus' suffering and death. The Messiah, of course, was not expected to be a *suffering* messiah. The facts of crucifixion and death jarred Jesus' followers into searching the Hebrew Scriptures for insight for proclaiming and interpreting his death (see the letter to the Hebrews, for example).[4]

Scholars tell us that what the Bible means by terms such as sacrifice and atonement may be quite different from the understandings that many of us have. For example, for Hebrew people, the blood of the sacrificed animal symbolized the life of the person or community. Pouring the blood on the altar was a symbolic gesture reuniting life with God. The sacrifices were an expression of the people's desire for reconciliation and union with God.[5]

It must be noted, however, that even while emphasizing these more positive meanings of sacrifice, most of the scholars pass over in silence the fact that the ritual still includes violence and the death of the victim, dimensions that are foreign to Jesus' vision of the reign of God.

Throughout the centuries Christians have reflected on and developed these different interpretations, leading to a variety of theologies and popular pieties, some of them quite distant from the Scriptures and even farther from the vision of Jesus.

In the fourth century, St. Augustine spoke of satisfaction for sin in legal terms of debts and justice. A key development took place in the eleventh century when the theologian St. Anselm used St. Augustine's ideas to describe atonement for sin. Anselm, reflecting the medieval culture of his day, understood sin to be something like a peasant insulting a king. Reconciliation would require satisfaction for this insult to the king's honor. Sin, however, is an infinite offense against God that demands adequate atonement. While humanity was obliged to atone, no human could pay this infinite debt. Only God could do so adequately.[6]

According to this eleventh-century view, that is exactly what Jesus, the God-Man, accomplished by his suffering and death. It was actually later theologians and preachers who added to Anselm's position by emphasizing blood and pain as the satisfaction that placated God's anger. Most Christians still grow up with such an understanding, although some are uneasy with this view, even if they do not know why.

This image of God — angry, demanding, even bloodthirsty — often appears in sermons, songs, and popular pieties today, although the focus is usually placed on Jesus' willingness to bear the suffering. Initially, this willingness to suffer for us may seem profoundly moving and consoling. But we must ask several questions of this interpretation. What does this say about God the Father? What kind of God could demand such torture of the beloved Son? Is this the God revealed by Jesus in his words and deeds?

Jesus Is Not Plan B

There is an alternative interpretation of the life and death of Jesus, also expressed in the Scriptures and throughout the tradition. This view, perhaps only on the margins of many people's religious understanding and devotion, is completely orthodox. Indeed, it offers perspectives much closer to Jesus' own experience and vision.

This alternative interpretation holds that the whole purpose of creation is for the incarnation, God's sharing of life and love in a unique and definitive way. God becoming human is not an afterthought, an event to make up for original sin and human sinfulness. Incarnation is God's first thought, the original design for all creation. The purpose of Jesus' life is the fulfillment of the whole creative process, of God's eternal longing to become human. Theologians call this the primacy of the incarnation.

For many of us who have lived a lifetime with the atonement view, it may be hard at first to hear this alternative, incarnational view. Yet it may offer some wonderful surprises for our relationship with God. God is not an angry or vindictive God, demanding the suffering and death of Jesus as payment for past sin. God is, instead, a gracious God, sharing divine life and love in creation and in the incarnation. Such a view can dramatically change our image of God, our approach to suffering, our day-to-day prayer. This approach is rooted solidly in the Fourth Gospel (SEE JOHN 1:1-18, 13:1–17:26) and in the letters to the Colossians and the Ephesians.

Throughout the centuries great Christian theologians have contributed to this positive perspective on God and Jesus. From the Cappadocian Fathers in the fourth century (St. Basil, St. Gregory of Nyssa, St. Gregory of Nazianzus) to Franciscan John Duns Scotus in the thirteenth century to Jesuits Teilhard de Chardin and Karl Rahner in the twentieth century, God's gracious love and the primacy of the incarnation have been proclaimed.[7] So, for example, Rahner states that "we can understand creation and incarnation as two moments and two phases of the *one* process of God's self-giving and self-expression, although it is an intrinsically differentiated process. Such an understanding can appeal to a very old 'Christocentric' tradition in the history of Christian theology in which the creative Word of God which establishes the world establishes this world to begin with as the materiality which is to become his own, or to become the environment of his own materiality."[8]

In the late twentieth century, theologian Catherine LaCugna pulled together many of these themes in her book *God for Us*. She uses and expands the Cappadocians' wonderful image of the Trinity as divine dance to include all persons. Borrowing themes of intimacy and communion from John's Gospel and Ephesians, she affirms that humanity has been made a partner in the divine dance, not through humanity's own merit but through God's election from all eternity. She writes:

> The God who does not need nor care for the creature, or who is immune to our suffering, does not exist. ... The God who keeps a ledger of our sins and failings, the divine policeman, does not exist. These are all false gods. ... What we believe about God must match what is revealed of God in Scripture: God watches over the widow and the poor, God makes the rains fall on just and unjust alike, God welcomes the stranger and embraces the enemy.[9]

Theologian Edward Schillebeeckx OP has also questioned the traditional interpretation of Jesus' death. In Part Four of his book *Christ*, Schillebeeckx strongly affirms and holds together God's goodness with suffering, both in Jesus' life and in all humans' experience. Schillebeeckx does not try to explain away the reality of suffering and evil in human history, but sees them as rooted in finitude and freedom. Still he stresses that God's mercy is greater, as seen in Jesus' ministry and teaching. God does not want people to suffer but wills to overcome suffering wherever it occurs.

Such a God could not require the death of Jesus. Schillebeeckx states: "*Negativity* cannot have a cause or a motive in God. But in that case we cannot look for a divine reason for the death of Jesus either. Therefore, first of all, we have to say that we are not redeemed *thanks* to the death of Jesus but *despite* it."[10] Schillebeeckx adds, "Nor will the Christian blasphemously claim that God himself required the death of Jesus as compensation for what we make of our history."[11]

Contemporary insights from Scripture scholars and from liberation theologians also affirm aspects of the alternative interpretation of Jesus' life and death. In his commentary on the crucifixion in Luke's gospel, Arthur Dewey emphasizes trust as the key to understanding this passage. Neither atonement nor sacrifice is even mentioned by Dewey. Rather, he notes that the early Jesus followers borrowed from Judaism the tradition of the suffering righteous one to make sense of Jesus' horrible death. "The innocent one was tried, mocked, and executed by evil men who wanted to find out whether the righteous one was truly a child of God. The vindication of the righteous one takes place, however, in God's space and time. Only from the point of view of faith can one perceive the true outcome."[12] Jesus' own trust in God is confirmed in the resurrection, the foundation of the followers' trust (faith). Dewey states that throughout the passage Luke points to the reign of God, "where trust alone has the final word."[13]

Writing in the general context of poverty and oppression in El Salvador and in the specific context of the 2001 earthquake, Jesuit Jon Sobrino addresses the ancient question of God and suffering (theodicy). He notes that some people (he calls them extremists) claimed that the earthquake was God's punishment for sin. He adds that an archbishop in Guatemala made a similar judgment after the earthquake there in 1976. Sobrino responds, however, calling this type of message "an insult to God" that is also "unjustly harmful to human beings" because it intensifies their spiritual anguish.[14]

Another reaction to the earthquake was simply submission, "God's will be done." Sobrino sees this response as understandable in El Salvador's traditional religious culture, but finally not satisfying, especially in the even more difficult times of civil war. Then the question was a profound "What's wrong with God?"[15]

Sobrino offers his own response, one that recognizes the mystery of God and suffering. "Our only choice, I believe, is to live with a theodicy unresolved in theory, and with a practice that goes on opening a pathway — with God walking it besides us — through the history of suffering."[16] Later he describes the theological foundation for this view while pondering the crucified God and the meaning of redemption: "It is the love of Jesus (and of God) that saves, not bloodshed. The love of Jesus saves human beings, especially victims; love that stays through to the end, even if it leads to a cross. That is what we call redemption. I think everyone can understand that, with no need for a sacrificial interpretation."[17]

What, then, can be said about Jesus' terrible death? Surely Jesus had to die, because he was human. However, he died by crucifixion because of human decree (the domination empire of his day) not by divine decree.

The emphasis on Jesus as God's first thought can free us from violent images of God and allows us to focus on God's overflowing love. This love is the very life of the Trinity and spills over into creation, incarnation, and the promise of fulfillment of all creation. What a difference this makes for our relationship with God! Life and love, not suffering and death, become the core of our spirituality and morality.

Into the Abyss

But what about the "dark abyss" (PSALM 88) of suffering? The incarnational approach with its emphasis on God's overflowing love leads us beyond our usual question of "Why?" and suggests three elements of a response to suffering: 1) acknowledge the suffering and then lament, 2) act, 3) trust in God.

We respond to suffering simply by being truthful, avoiding denial, and admitting the pain and horror of the suffering, whatever the cause. We must never glorify suffering. Yes, it can lead us to deeper maturity and wisdom, but suffering can also crush the human spirit. The first step to grief and healing, then, is to move from overwhelmed silence to speech, the bold speech of lament. The Psalms show us how to speak out against suffering and oppression, even against God. But such crying out allows us both to grieve and to grow into a mature covenant partner with God. A paraphrase of Psalm 56 expresses well this relationship: "Be gracious to us, O God. Enter our lament in your book. Store every tear in your flask."

Awareness of suffering and relationship with God allow and inspire our action. We acknowledge that at times our choices have caused personal and social suffering, so one form of action is moving toward repentance and a change of heart. We also suffer from sickness and many other personal challenges. In this suffering we need to reach out to others, to ask for help, to receive what they offer, to allow them to accompany us in the dark abyss.

Following the life and ministry of Jesus, we also work as individuals and as communities to overcome and end suffering. We know that some suffering results from persons' evil choices (war, injustice, oppression). We know that other suffering simply happens in a world that is not yet fulfilled (earthquakes, debilitating diseases). Our deeds include remaining with others in their suffering, along with action concerning political and economic issues. We cannot do everything, but we can and must do at least one thing, whatever God asks of us.[18]

The third element in our response to suffering, trust in God, is of course especially challenging in the dark times of suffering. Jesus, as we have seen, is a marvelous example of trust in God. His deep, trusting relationship with *Abba* grounded his life and teaching and sustained him in his suffering. "Are not two sparrows sold for a penny? Yet not one of them will fall to the ground apart from your Father. And even the hairs of your head are all counted. So do not be afraid; you are of more value than many sparrows" (MATT 10:29-31). We follow Jesus' words and life by entrusting our lives to our God who has been called a Loving Abyss.[19]

Our God suffers with us, to use human terms. In the depths of suffering we too may cry out: "My God, my God, why have your forsaken me?" (MATT 27:46; MARK 15:34) In the darkness, we may need to express our lament, even defiance, but finally our trust that the gracious, gentle God holds our suffering bodies and spirits. How could it be otherwise for the God of life, the covenanted partner, the tender and gracious parent, the infinite abyss of love?

God does not desire suffering but works to overcome it. God did not demand Jesus' suffering and does not want ours. In the context of trusting this gentle God, we lament and act to overcome suffering, even as we acknowledge its incomprehensibility and marvel at God's remarkable respect of human freedom. Suffering remains a mystery, not a problem to be solved. We move past "Why?" to ask instead: "How can I respond? What can we do now?" A profound trust in a compassionate God allows us to ask these questions and then to act, with surprising peace and hope.

We can trust because there is even more: our God is a God of resurrection, of new life. Jesus' story did not end with suffering and death, but with new and transformed life. Trust in God is not some pie-in-the-sky piety, but a profound conviction rooted in the experience of the risen Jesus. Christians are an Easter people, trusting that good overcomes evil, that life overcomes death. Christians trust that God leads us as individuals and as community in resisting evil and brings us all to the fullness of life.

ENDNOTES

1. Pheme Perkins, "The Gospel of Mark," in *The New Interpreter's Bible* (Nashville: Abingdon, 1995), Volume VIII, 544-45.

2. For more details, see Daniel Harrington, *Why Do We Suffer?* (Franklin, Wis: Sheed & Ward, 2000), 15-29.

3. John H. Elliott, "Patronage and Clientism in Early Christian Society," *Forum*, vol 3, no 4 (December 1987), 39-48. Arthur J. Dewey, "The Truth That Is in Je-

sus," *The Fourth R*, vol 16, no 4 (July-August 2003), 7-11. Edward Schillebeeckx, *Jesus: An Experiment in Christology* (New York: Seabury, 1979), 256-71.

4. Arthur J. Dewey, "Can We Let Jesus Die?" in *The Once & Future Faith*, Robert W. Funk and the Jesus Seminar, (Santa Rosa, Polebridge, 2001), 135-59.

5. Anthony J. Tambasco, *A Theology of Atonement and Paul's Vision of Christianity* (Collegeville: Liturgical, 1991), 65-71.

6. Michael Winter, *The Atonement* (Collegeville: Liturgical, 1995), 61-79. See also: Lisa Sowle Cahill, "The Atonement Paradigm," *Theological Studies*, 68 (2007), 418-32.

7. For more on the Cappadocians, see Catherine LaCugna, *God for Us* (New York: HarperSanFrancisco, 1991), 53-79 and 270-278; on John Duns Scotus, see B.M. Bonaseo OFM, *Man and His Approach to God in John Duns Scotus* (Lanham, Md: UP of America, 1983), 44-50; on Teilhard de Chardin, see Christopher Mooney SJ, *Teilhard de Chardin and the Mystery of Christ* (New York: Harper & Row, 1966), 133-145; on Karl Rahner, see William Dych, *Karl Rahner* (Collegeville: Liturgical, 1992), 65-81.

8. Karl Rahner, *Foundations of Christian Faith* (New York: Seabury, 1978), 197.

9. LaCugna, *God for Us*, 397.

10. Edward Schillebeeckx, *Christ: The Experience of Jesus as Lord* (New York: Seabury, 1980), 729.

11. Ibid., 728.

12. Arthur Dewey, *The Word in Time* (revised edition) (New Berlin, Wis.: Liturgical Publications, 1990), 216.

13. Ibid., 217.

14. Jon Sobrino, *Where is God? Earthquake, Terrorism, Barbarity, and Hope* (Maryknoll: Orbis, 2004), 138.

15. Ibid., 139-40.

16. Ibid., 142.

17. Ibid., 148.

18. For a profound reflection on this insight, see Walter Wink, *Engaging the Powers* (Minneapolis: Fortress, 1992), 304-8.

19. Karl Rahner SJ speaks of God as Holy Mystery, the Incomprehensible One, a Loving Abyss. See, for example, "Why Am I a Christian Today?'" in *The Practice of Faith* (New York: Crossroad, 1986), 8; also "Thoughts on the Possibility of Belief Today" in *Theological Investigations*, vol V (Baltimore: Helicon, 1966), 8-9.

CHAPTER 14

End-of-Life Ethics

Preparing Now for the Hour of Death

Have you ever said to your family, "Don't put me on all those life-support machines and tubes"? Perhaps you had just visited a friend in the hospital or were simply reacting to stories such as those about Terri Schiavo, the Floridian who lived on life support for years before that life support was removed in 2005 in the midst of a national debate. Perhaps you had a sense that the life-support machines were not so much promoting life but, rather, simply delaying death. As a result, you are convinced that you don't want to be in that situation.

Or perhaps you reacted very differently to experiences like Terry Schiavo's death. You are convinced that feeding tubes must be used. Perhaps you found yourself confused by the debate, disagreement, and polarization. You are wondering what faithful Catholics ought to do about these ethical issues and what role, if any, the government ought to play.

End-of-life issues touch the depths of our being, stir the emotions, and raise profound questions. They call for careful moral reasoning. In this chapter, we will look to the Hebrew and Christian Scriptures and to insights from our long Catholic tradition for guidance and wisdom in making moral decisions. We will suggest appropriate responses for us as faithful disciples of Jesus and as concerned citizens. We'll also consider what we can do now for the hour of *our* death by filling out an advance directive (a living will or healthcare power of attorney).

Words of Wisdom

The Scriptures provide a foundation and a sure direction in helping us to respond to end-of-life questions by offering three major points: (1) life is a basic, but not absolute, good, (2) we are to be stewards of life, but we don't have complete control, and (3) we understand death in the context of belief in new life.

In the Creation story in Genesis, we hear of the goodness of all creation (GEN 1:31) and, in a special way, the sacredness of all human life, for we are created in God's image (1:27). Human life, then, possesses a dignity, rooted in *who we are*, rather than in *what we do*. Life is holy, deserving of respect and reverence. We know from experience that life is the foundation for all other goods: friendship, love, prayer, and all the other ways we enjoy and serve God and neighbor.

Life, however, is not an absolute good. There is a greater good: our relationship with God. We would not, for example, destroy our relationship with God through sin in order to save our physical life. The powerful witness of martyrs — and especially Jesus — testifies to this truth.

Stewardship, our second major point, must be distinguished from dominion. Stewardship implies that we have the responsibility to care for something that is not totally our own possession. Dominion, on the other hand, claims an ultimate control. Life, as we have already seen, is a gift of God, to be respected and reverenced. Jesus' whole life modeled the idea of stewardship, creatively nourishing the gift of life (SEE JOHN 6:22–71).

The third point that the Scriptures offer us is the conviction that death marks the transformation to new and eternal life. This belief does not deny the reality of death, along with its suffering and separation. Yet life is changed, not ended. Our belief in everlasting life is rooted, of course, in the transforming experience of the resurrection of Jesus (SEE LUKE 24:1-53; JOHN 20:1–21:25). We, too, trust in God's loving faithfulness.

Euthanasia and Assisted Suicide

How, then do these three insights — life is a basic good, we are stewards of life, death is not the final word — enlighten end-of-life issues? How do they help us to sort through the dilemmas of euthanasia, assisted suicide, treatment, and use of life-support systems? The conviction that we are stewards of life grounds the opposition to euthanasia. We use our creativity to cure illness, but we also acknowledge that ultimately death cannot be avoided. As stewards, we respond with care and compassion to those who are suffering. Indeed, we have much to learn about better methods of pain control. Mercy killing *seems* to offer a solution to profound human fears: the fear of dying, of losing control, of being a burden, of being strapped with terrible pain. Mercy killing, however, moves beyond stewardship into dominion. Euthanasia, even for compassionate reasons, implies that we have absolute control over life and so contradicts who we are as faithful stewards of God's gift of life.

Similarly, with assisted suicide, recognizing both the good gift of life and our responsibilities as stewards prohibits choosing suicide or helping someone else to end his or her life. Assisted suicide, though rooted in frustration, pain, or despair, speaks of dominion, of attempting to seize ultimate control over life. It, too, contradicts the fundamental reality of our lives and so undermines our humanity.

Both of these decisions may seem to be very private decisions, yet they have profound implications for society. Many Church groups and others see that legalizing euthanasia and assisted suicide would further undermine reverence for life in our society, would reduce trust in the medical profession, and would put old and infirm people in very vulnerable positions. The public policy dimensions of the euthanasia issue are very serious and demand an intelligent, nuanced response that respects the dignity of all persons.

Treatment and Life Support

Questions about the use of medical treatments and life-support systems are distinct from—and yet often associated with—euthanasia. The scriptural insights can be very helpful with these issues even if they cannot give details. As good stewards, we believe that death is not the final word, that life is not an absolute good. Therefore, we do not have to keep someone alive "at all costs."

The Catholic tradition helps with the details, providing this guidance: ordinary means must be used; extraordinary means are optional. Ordinary means are medicines or treatments that offer reasonable hope of benefit and can be used without excessive expense, pain, or other inconvenience. Extraordinary means do not offer reasonable hope of benefit or include excessive expense, pain, or other inconvenience. What is important to remember is that "ordinary" and "extraordinary" refer not to the technology but to the treatment *in relation* to the condition of the patient, that is, to the proportion of benefit and burden the treatment provides the patient.[1]

Many people remember when Cardinal Joseph Bernardin of Chicago decided to stop the treatment for his cancer. The treatment had become extraordinary. He did not kill himself by this choice but did stop efforts that prolonged his dying. He allowed death to occur. (This distinction between allowing to die and killing, as in euthanasia or assisted suicide, is of great significance in the Catholic tradition. The rejection of this distinction by several U.S. courts raises serious concerns.)

Within the Catholic Church, debate still surrounds the question of providing medical nourishment through a feeding tube. Let's look at two positions:

1. "Life must almost always be sustained." This position holds that the withdrawal of medically assisted nutrition and hydration cannot be ethically justified except in very rare situations. The fundamental idea for this position is the following: remaining alive is never rightly regarded as a burden because human bodily life is inherently good, not merely instrumental to other goods. Therefore, it is rarely morally right not to provide adequate food and fluids.

This position acknowledges that means of preserving life may be withheld or withdrawn if the means employed is judged either useless or excessively burdensome. The "useless or excessive burden" criteria can be applied to the person who is imminently dying but not to those who are permanently unconscious or to those who require medically assisted nutrition and hydration as a result of something like Lou Gehrig's or Alzheimer's disease. Providing these patients with medical nourishment by means of tubes is not useless because it does bring these patients a great benefit: namely, the preservation of their lives.

2. "Life is a fundamental but not absolute good." This approach rejects euthanasia, judging deliberate killing a violation of human dignity. On the other hand, while it values life as a great and fundamental good, life is not seen as an absolute (as we saw in the section on scriptural foundations) to be sustained in every situation. Accordingly, in some situations, medically assisted nutrition and hydration may be removed.

This position states that the focus on imminent death may be misplaced. Instead we should ask whether a disease or condition that will lead to death (a fatal pathology) is present. For example, a patient in a persistent vegetative state cannot eat enough to live and thus will die of that pathology in a short time unless life-prolonging devices are used. Withholding medically assisted hydration and nutrition from a patient in such a state does not cause a new fatal disease or condition. It simply allows an already existing fatal pathology to take its natural course.

Here, then, is a fundamental idea of this position: if a fatal condition is present, the ethical question we must ask is whether there is a moral obligation to seek to remove or bypass the fatal pathology. But how do we decide either to treat a fatal pathology or to let it take its natural course? Life is a great and fundamental good, a necessary condition for pursuing life's purposes: happiness, fulfillment, love of God and neighbor.

But does the obligation to prolong life ever cease? Yes, says this view, if prolonging life does not help the person strive for the purposes of life. Pursuing life's purposes implies some ability to function at the level of reasoning, relating, and communicating. If efforts to restore this cognitive-affective function can be judged useless or would result in profound frustration (that is, a severe burden) in pursuing the purposes of life, then the ethical obligation to prolong life is no longer present.

Disagreements in the Church

How are these significantly different positions judged by the Roman Catholic Church? There is no definitive Catholic position regarding these two approaches. Vatican commissions and Catholic bishops' conferences have come down on both sides of the issue. Likewise, there are Catholic moral theologians on both sides.

In an attempt to respond to this controversy in 1992, the Committee for Pro-life Activities of the National Conference of Catholic Bishops (now the USCCB) issued *Nutrition and Hydration: Moral and Pastoral Reflections.* This statement called for a presumption in favor of using medically assisted nutrition and hydration, but added that it may be removed in certain circumstances, e.g., when burdens outweigh benefits. This guidance was then included in the bishops' *Ethical and Religious Directives for Catholic Health Care Services.*

In 2004, Pope John Paul II, speaking at a Vatican conference, seemed to disagree with the U.S. bishops' statements by opposing the removal of medically assisted nutrition and hydration ("seemed" because there is debate about whether the pope allowed removal in some circumstances). In 2007 the Congregation for the Doctrine of the Faith (CDF) responded to specific questions concerning the use of artificial nutrition and hydration for patients in a persistent vegetative state (PVS). In light of its interpretation of John Paul's statement, the CDF wrote: "The administration of food and water even by artificial means is, in principle, an ordinary and proportionate means of preserving life." Then in 2009, the U.S. bishops revised their *Ethical and Religious Directives for Catholic Health Care Services* to reflect this judgment.

Although these statements seem to affirm the "Life must almost always be sustained view," responsible Catholic moralists, including those involved in Catholic health care, have argued that the balancing of burdens and benefits is still present. They judge that the CDF's position contains inconsistencies (because Church teaching does permit the removal of respirators) and seems to come close to idolizing biological life by making it an absolute value. These moral theologians note that the CDF statement applies only to PVS patients. They also point out that all these statements deserve proper respect but that they are not infallible pronouncements. So disagreements continue.[2]

Advance Directives

Suffering, moral questions, and legal implications make death-and-dying situations so very difficult. What can we do to make our wishes known now for the time when we are no longer capable of making health-care decisions for ourselves? We can reflect and pray, discuss with our families and physicians, and indicate in writing our desires for health care by creating an advance directive.

There are two different types. The first type of document is the *living will*, a statement prepared in advance so that people, while competent, can direct their families and physicians concerning the type of treatment they want (or do not want) should they become terminally ill and incompetent. The living will is recognized as a legal document.

On the other hand, the living will, by its nature being a document prepared in advance, may be seen as making a decision before the concrete situation has been faced. Because no one can foresee all the details of a future illness and medical procedures, the living will is limited but at least offers some reflection and foresight to the types of treatment desired.

The second type of document is the *healthcare power of attorney*. In this document, an individual gives another person the legal authority to make healthcare decisions when he or she is no longer able to do so. The decisions made by the appointed person (technically called an "attorney-in-fact" or sometimes "proxy" or "surrogate"; this person need not be an attorney-at-law) are based on the current medical condition of the patient and on the patient's previously expressed desires concerning treatment.

As a result, this form of dealing with dying-and-death situations seems to be preferable. It provides both for respect for the individual's desires concerning treatment and for current informed consent made by the attorney-in-fact who knows—after careful consultation with doctors, nurses, and chaplains—the specific medical options facing the patient. It does not rely merely on a previously written statement to cover all possible situations.

In appointing someone to act on your behalf, clearly you will choose someone you trust (e.g., a spouse, son, daughter, best friend) to be the attorney-in-fact, someone with whom you have carefully discussed your wishes concerning treatment. Because laws vary from state to state, it is wise to consult a lawyer about both types of documents. Your physician may also be able to help you. Communication with your family and doctor is also an essential part of the process.

The Final Mystery of Life

Advance directives are for everyone of legal age, not just senior citizens. If this seems to you like too much effort, it is not! The whole process of planning now for the hour of death is a concrete way to express your care and love for your family and friends. It will allow them to know your desires clearly, especially since they will be the ones faced with the difficult and painful decisions. It lessens the possibility of friction or guilt feelings about relationships that frequently cause difficulties in such situations.

Planning now is also a responsible consideration of the appropriate use of the earth's resources. Certainly your decisions about types of treatment will have implications for costs, care, and use of scarce medical resources. Finally, planning now can be a prayerful experience, confronting the final mystery of life and trusting in our gracious God, the source and goal of all life.

ENDNOTES

1. See the Vatican's *Declaration on Euthanasia*, IV, 1980.
2. For an article rich in context, nuance, and insight, read Daniel Sulmasy's "Preserving Life?" in *Commonweal*, Volume CXXXIV, Number 21; 7 December 2007.

CHAPTER 15

Loving God, Holy Mystery

Multiplying Our Images of God

In the hospital's intensive care unit, I sat next to a dying Jesuit friend. I knew he was falling into the abyss of death, yet I also "knew" he would be OK, because ultimately he was falling into the loving abyss of God.

God, the Alpha and Omega, the beginning and end of all life, is the center of every believer's life. But how can we speak of God?[1] What images do we find helpful in trying to describe that which cannot be fully described? What is *your* favorite image of God? What do we say of God in times of suffering?

Relationship with God is the heart of our spiritual-moral life. The images we have of God play an important role in how this relationship develops. If, as we grew up, we were taught about a God who judges and punishes us, then our relationship might be characterized by fear or even avoidance. If, instead, God's love and forgiveness had been emphasized, we probably have a very different relationship with God, one characterized by warmth and acceptance.

The Eucharist and other sacraments and private prayer continue to influence our images of God and so shape our relationship. Other experiences, past and present, also influence how we think and feel about God, for example, if we had an abusive father or if we have experienced a deep and unconditional love. Suffering frequently raises profound questions about God: "Why did God do this?" or even "Is there a God?"

A wise Scripture scholar[2] once said that we need to *multiply* our images of God. Different images help us to appreciate different aspects of God, who is always greater than any one description. But each image can give us a glimpse of the Holy Mystery, the source and goal of all life, and so nurture our relationship with God.

The Bible itself offers us a wonderful variety of images of God, including fire, shepherd, warrior, shelter, light, bread of life, love, the Holy One. Two that we may take for granted are woman and man: God created humans in God's image; in the divine image God created them; male and female God created them (SEE GEN 1:27). Human beings are icons of God.

One perhaps surprising image is God as rock! Listen to the psalmist: "I love you, O LORD, my strength. The LORD is my rock, my fortress, and my deliverer, my God, my rock in whom I take refuge" (Ps 18:1-2). "[God] alone is my rock and my salvation, my fortress; I shall never be shaken" (Ps 62:2). Hardly an image of tenderness or compassion! Yet the psalmist is comfortable calling God a rock. The prophet Isaiah also: "Trust in the LORD forever! For the LORD is an eternal rock" (Is 26:4).

Other passages in the Bible speak of God in maternal terms. "You forgot the God who gave you birth" (DEUT 32:18). Similarly, the unknown prophet known as Second Isaiah with the people in exile had God ask, "Can a mother forget her infant, be without tenderness for the child of her womb? Even should she forget, I will never forget you" (Is 49:15). In the Wisdom literature especially (SEE WIS 7:7–8:8 FOR EXAMPLE) and throughout the Bible there are many feminine references and images, some based on biological activity (such as giving birth) and others on women's cultural activities (such as being a midwife).

The prophet Hosea describes God as a gentle parent. "When Israel was a child I loved him, out of Egypt I called my son. The more I called them, the farther they went from me.... Yet it was I who taught Ephraim to walk, who took them in my arms; I drew them with human cords, with bands of love" (Hos 11:1-4).

Jesus calls God *Abba* ("Daddy") and two of his parables pair feminine and masculine images of God: a woman looking for a lost coin and a father looking for a lost son (SEE LUKE 15). These and other parables and teachings point to an intimate, loving relationship with a merciful and faithful God.

All these biblical images of God may help us to appreciate characteristics of God like gentle compassion, faithfulness, strength, love. Still, along with the images must come some caution. "If we use words hewn from the things around us for God, we reduce [God] to a thing around us."[3] God is always more, always other. God is neither male nor female, neither shepherd nor rock!

In many of his writings, theologian Karl Rahner, S.J., offers a different kind of image and so helps us to think carefully about the reality behind all images. He never ceases to remind us that God is more than we can ever explain or articulate. God is Holy Mystery, the Incomprehensible One, the Loving Abyss.

In the chapter on Rahner in her *Quest for the Living God*, Elizabeth Johnson concisely presents the heart of Rahner's insight. "This one holy mystery is the ineffable God who while remaining eternally a plentitude — infinite, incomprehensible, inexpressible — wishes to self-communicate to the world, and does so in the historically tangible person of Jesus Christ and in the grace of the Spirit so as to become the blessedness of every person and of the universe itself."[4]

Johnson spells out this remarkable sentence emphasizing two parts: God's transcendence and God's immanence. Transcendence speaks of

God's otherness, always greater and more, not a particular being (like you and I and all other creatures) but the ground of being (Unlimited Being). Because God is transcendent, God can be immanent, meaning intimate nearness, within all that is.

God's self-communication has taken place in Jesus, "the human person in whom God's irrevocable union with humanity in self-giving love is decisively achieved and revealed."[5] God's self-communication also takes place in the Spirit given directly to all human beings — what we call grace.

Despite his emphasis on God as mystery, Rahner still uses aspects of our physical world to point us in the right direction. Those who live near an ocean (or have visited one) experience the endless immensity of the water when looking out toward the horizon. Rahner comments that we humans are "forever occupied with the grains of sand along the shore" where we dwell "at the edge of the infinite ocean of mystery."[6] Sitting at the edge of the Grand Canyon and peering into the depths can also help make real the meaning of an abyss.

Rahner's emphasis on Holy Mystery may be especially helpful in times of doubt, darkness, and suffering. In the distant past the Psalmist described suffering as a dark abyss (PSALM 88); Rahner describes God as a loving abyss, an abyss deserving our awe, wonder, and worship.

First he speaks of Jesus' experience of the abyss:

> There is Jesus, a human being who loves, who is faithful unto death, in whom all of human existence, life, speech and action, is open to the mystery which he calls his Father and to which he surrenders in confidence even when all is lost. For him the immeasurable dark abyss of his life is the Father's protecting hand. And so he holds fast to love for human beings and also to his one hope even when everything seems to be being destroyed in death, when it no longer seems possible to love God and human beings.[7]

Then Rahner turns to his own experience:

> What could I put in the place of Christianity? Only emptiness, despair, night, and death. And what reason do I have to consider this abyss as truer and more real than the abyss of God? It is easier to let oneself fall into one's own emptiness than into the abyss of the Blessed Mystery. But it is not more courageous or truer. This truth, of course, shines out only when it is also loved and accepted since it is the truth which makes us free and whose light consequently begins to shine only in the freedom which dares all to the very height.... [This truth] gives me the courage to believe in it and to call to it when all the dark despairs and lifeless voids would swallow me up.[8]

Multiplying our images of God can enrich and enliven our relationship with God. The image beyond other images—God as Holy Mystery, Loving Abyss—captures the wonder of God and offers hope and light in times of doubt and darkness, especially as we sit at the edge of death.

ENDNOTES

1. See "Within the Holy Mystery" by Michael J. Buckley, S.J. in *A World of Grace*, edited by Leo O'Donovan, S.J., New York: Crossroad, 1987, pp. 31-49.

2. Barbara E. Bowe, R.S.C.J. See her *Biblical Foundations of Spirituality*, Lanham: Rowman & Littlefield, 2003.

3. Buckley, p. 41.

4. Elizabeth Johnson, *Quest for the Living God*, New York: Continuum, 2007, p. 43.

5. Otto H. Hentz, S.J., "Anticipating Jesus Christ: An Account of our Hope" in O'Donovan, p. 113.

6. Karl Rahner, S.J., "The Experience of God Today" in *Theological Investigations* XI, New York: Seabury Press, 1974, p. 159.

7. Karl Rahner, S.J., "Why Am I a Christian Today?" in *The Practice of Faith*, New York: Crossroad, 1986, p. 8.

8. Karl Rahner, S.J., "Thoughts on the Possibility of Belief Today" in *Theological Investigations* V, Baltimore: Helicon Press, 1966, pp. 8-9.

EPILOGUE

Turning Point

Encountering John the Baptist

Peru and its people changed my life and ministry. In 1972, the year before I was ordained, six of us from Jesuit School of Theology in Chicago spent our summer in Peru. The opportunity to study, travel, see, and listen offered us an experience of "conscientization" (transforming awareness). We met with generals and bishops, pastors and students, the poor and the wealthy to learn about Peruvian reality.

Throughout the country, we encountered profound poverty. Questions of human dignity and justice, ethics and economics, the mystery of God and suffering stretched my worldview.

I returned to the U.S., wrestling with how I might best "help souls" (one of St. Ignatius Loyola's favorite phrases for describing the work of the Society of Jesus; he meant the whole person). Going to Peru after ordination did not seem my path. Instead I chose to study for a Ph.D. in Christian ethics, focusing on social justice. I have now spent many years at Xavier University in Cincinnati teaching and publishing about all the fundamental questions I experienced in Peru.

Some years ago I returned to Peru and revisited Villa El Salvador, a shantytown established in 1971 where we had lived briefly. Now looking out over a sprawling area with hundreds of thousands of people, I realized that so much of my life — my ministry, my worldview, the majority of people in my life, my sense of God — was different because of Peru. I asked how appropriately I had responded to this amazing gift, and I cried tears of wonder and gratitude.

When I returned from Peru after this experience, I continued to ponder what it all meant for my life and faith. A wise retreat director suggested that I consider Jesus' return to the Jordan where John baptized — and where, according to the synoptic gospels, Jesus himself had been baptized. John's gospel does not mention Jesus being baptized by John, but it does include various details also found in the accounts in Mark, Matthew, and Luke, such as the Spirit descending on Jesus and John the Baptist's testimony about Jesus. The story of Jesus' return to this specific spot "across the Jordan" is found only in John's gospel (10:40-42).

I reflected on both scenes—Jesus with John at the Jordan and then Jesus' later return to that place. Jesus' baptism evidently was a very special experience for the early communities to remember it. In some ways, though, the baptism must have been seen as an embarrassment to the followers of Jesus. How could it be that Jesus, Messiah and Lord, needed to be or at least chose to be baptized? Perhaps this is why the gospel of John omits the baptism altogether.

The gospels' descriptions of John the Baptist and Jesus, of course, are told from the perspective of Jesus' followers. At the time, John was better known. Both had disciples, and there must have been competition on both sides to "set the record straight." All this makes the synoptic gospels' accounts of Jesus being baptized by John even more remarkable.

So why was this event remembered and handed on? Perhaps because of its significance for Jesus' understanding of his life and vision for his ministry. Taking seriously that Jesus was fully human (as the Church teaches—and also fully divine) I recognized that Jesus had to discern his life's path just like we all do. His encounter with John and the baptism must have marked a turning point in Jesus' life, giving him a deepening sense of being God's "beloved," called to live and proclaim Abba God's loving presence, the Reign of God. The specifics of all this would have to be worked out and confirmed in the doing. In all four gospels, the stories of Jesus and John the Baptist mark the beginning of Jesus' public ministry.

Then, when Jesus' words and deeds eventually led to conflict and threats of arrest and even stoning (JOHN 10:31, 39), Jesus returns to where his ministry began. Was he looking back to the first experience and wondering how he in fact had responded? Was he questioning it all? Was he searching for confirmation, for renewed commitment, for new life and energy? John's gospel simply says that "many there began to believe in him" (10:42).

Peru and its people were John the Baptist for me. The first encounter transformed my vision of life and ministry, turning my attention to structural injustices and raising the age-old question of how to hold together suffering and a gracious God. When I returned many years later, I asked myself (and others) about my response to that first significant encounter. After years of everyday work as a professor of theology, with both achievements and failures, affirmations and conflicts, I reviewed and evaluated my efforts for the poor and marginalized. I prayed for deepening trust in the God of compassion and nonviolence revealed by Jesus, searching for renewed energy and commitment. How best to continue "helping souls" now?

I wonder whether encounters with John the Baptist throughout the liturgical cycle can be for others as they now are for me: a reminder of a significant turning point in life. Can they also evoke a return in search of renewed consolation and creativity in serving others, along with the desire for a more intimate relationship with our God of life and love?

Other books from Lectio you may like...

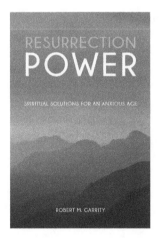

CPSIA information can be obtained
at www.ICGtesting.com
Printed in the USA
LVHW081210051218
599279LV00010B/48/P